CAS WALKER

CAS WALKER

Stories on His Life and Legend

★ ★ ★

EDITED BY
Joshua S. Hodge

The University of Tennessee Press ★ Knoxville

Copyright © 2019 by The University of Tennessee Press / Knoxville.
All Rights Reserved. Manufactured in the United States of America.
First Edition.

Library of Congress Cataloging-in-Publication Data

Names: Hodge, Joshua S., editor.
Title: Cas Walker: stories on his life and legend / edited by Joshua S. Hodge.
Description: First edition. | Knoxville: The University of Tennessee Press, [2019] | Includes bibliographical references and index. |
Identifiers: LCCN 2019013799 (print) | LCCN 2019014572 (ebook) | ISBN 9781621905363 (pdf) | ISBN 9781621905356 (pbk.)
Subjects: LCSH: Walker, Cas. | Politicians—Tennessee—Knoxville—Biography. | Businessmen—Tennessee—Knoxville—Biography. | Knoxville (Tenn.)—Biography.
Classification: LCC F444.K7 (ebook) | LCC F444.K7 C37 2019 (print) | DDC 324.2092 [B] —dc23
LC record available at https://lccn.loc.gov/2019013799

I think he will always be talked about. Good or bad, I don't know—
but I think as time goes on, there will be more stories about him, because
people that were there and dealt with him directly are gonna be gone.

And some of the people will be sitting around: "This is what I heard. . . .
This is what I heard."

"This man couldn't have been like that! This man couldn't have done
that!"

But he did! He did. That's what attracted me to him.

He'd go somewhere, and crowds—you could see them: "Cas is gonna
be here!"

I'd go to that store on Magnolia, because it was closer to me. "Cas is
gonna be out in the parking lot this afternoon at 2:00!"

"Doing what?"

"Just be out in the parking lot talking to people."

And people would come from all over, just to see him, me included.

I'd get across the street on a little bank, and sit there for thirty, forty
minutes waiting on him. I couldn't hear what he was saying, he was
across the street. Just to see him.

—JACK SHARP, Knoxville City Councilman

CONTENTS

Acknowledgments — xi

Introduction. Cas Walker, Knoxville, and the American Century — 1

Chapter 1. "I Never Did Try to Act Better Than Anybody": Scenes from Cas Walker's Early Life — 7

Chapter 2. "If I'd Thought of a Few More Things, I'd Have Stooped a Little Lower": Selling Groceries — 15

Chapter 3. "Digger O'Dell–Buried Alive" — 39

Chapter 4. "I Work for Cas Walker" — 47

Chapter 5. "The Guy Literally Was Everywhere": A Pioneer of Radio and TV — 55

Chapter 6. "Cash" Walker, Benefactor — 75

Chapter 7. Bare-Knuckle Politics — 93

Chapter 8. Cas on Communism and Civil Rights — 121

Chapter 9. "The Ole Coon Hunter" — 133

Chapter 10. The *Watchdog*: "The Unvarnished Naked Truth That Can Be Backed Up in Court" — 143

Chapter 11. Troubles — 159

Epilogue. The Legacy of Cas Walker — 179

Contributors — 193

Bibliography — 195

Index of Names — 197

ILLUSTRATIONS

Sketch of Walker's First Store at 1100 E. Vine Avenue	10
Cas with Mules on the "Farm and Home Hour"	57
Cas Sworn In as Mayor of Knoxville, April 17, 1959	95
"Swearing-In Ceremony," by Charlie Daniels	98
Mary Pat Tyree, Cas Walker, and Randy Tyree, May 19, 1981	100
Fistfight at the City Council, March 1956	104
Cas with Stuffed Raccoon, December 17, 1981	136
Attorney W.P. Boone Dougherty and Cas Walker, c. 1981	153
Cas Walker and U.S. Marshal Quarles, c. 1960	161
Walker Makes Amends with Dave Gaddis and Gene Morrell	163
Mary H. Tindell with Robert Ritchie, July 2, 1971	164
Cas and Virginia "Ginny" Walker, date unknown	172

Following page 109
Cas Walker Bands, ca. 1950s–60
Cas Walker on the Children's Bus, ca. 1940s
Cas's Family
Mayor Walker with Orange Bowl Queen, c. 1945
Cas during Tax Evasion Trial, c. 1961
Cas after Being Acquitted, c. 1961
Cas Sworn In as Councilman, January 1964
Cas Walker Motions to "Speak Up!"
Fire at Walker's Magnolia Avenue Store, c. 1924
Cas Walker On Trial, c. 1981
Cas Walker, "Straighten," c. 1985
Cas Walker's Final Resting Place, Woodlawn Cemetery,
　September 28, 1998

ACKNOWLEDGMENTS

Many people and institutions have contributed to this project. I am so pleased to take a moment to thank everyone who provided stories, insights, and commentary about Cas Walker. However, any and all mistakes within these pages are my own.

First and foremost, this book is the culmination of an idea Ernest Freeberg had years ago. I have been very fortunate to be the beneficiary of his superb intellect and am thankful to have him as a leader, confidant, and friend. His financial, intellectual, and moral support has cultivated my confidence as a scholar and enhanced this project in numerous ways. Without Dr. Freeberg, this book would not exist.

The people of Knoxville have also greatly enriched this book. A special thanks to Victor Ashe, Betty Bean, Robert "Bob" Booker, James Bragg, Becky Orange Dwarshius, Bennie Wallen Jean, Bob Lutrell, Larry Mathis, Zimbabwe Motavou, Bo Pierce, Bradley Reeves, Doug "Rowdy Cope" Rutherford, Jack Sharp, Julia Tucker, Randy Tyree, Ben H. Walker, Carl Warner, David West, Bruce Wheeler, and Jack Wiedemann. I spent many hours conversing with these interviewees and thoroughly enjoyed their company, even beyond their knowledge of Cas Walker. Included in this book of stories are also several previously published articles. The works of Betty Bean, Ray Jenkins, Bill Maples, Jacquelyn B. McClary, and Sam Venable contextualize the life of Cas Walker.

While conducting interviews in the summer of 2016, Bean published a short article that promoted our project to Knoxville readers and invited people to submit their own stories. In response, a variety of people contacted the UT History Department with written submissions that helped illuminate some of the more evasive events in Walker's life. For their submissions, I would like to thank Carter G. Baker, David Correll, Louie Chester

Finley, Ernie Gannon, Diana Hawk, Julia Rose, Jeff Ross, Bill Routh, Jane Bandy Shuler, and Jerry Wing.

The UT History Department supported this endeavor in many ways also, including task-oriented support, purchase of digital equipment, and summer internships. Graduate student Jake Nelson did the painstaking work of transcribing our oral histories for the book, for which I am forever grateful. Josh Jeffery also used ocular character recognition software to reproduce many publications regarding Walker. Such support from the department and from my colleagues has enhanced the range of stories that are included in this book.

Operating from different Knoxville institutions, Cherel Henderson, Lisa Oakley, Steve Cotham, Jack McElroy, and Georgianna Vines have all contributed to this book. Henderson and Oakley provided ample space within the East Tennessee History Center for several interviews. In addition to providing genealogical charts of Walker's family, Henderson also arranged an important discussion with David West, the longtime driver and band member who accompanied Walker through his last decades. Many of the images from this book come from the Calvin M. McClung Collections, curated by Steve Cotham. Cotham provided access to a range of Walker files and his comments on the manuscript spurred changes that brought much clarity to this book's narrative. In addition, Jack McElroy, editor of the Knoxville News Sentinel, offered the newspaper's images of Walker that have survived into the twenty-first century. While this book focuses on recorded interviews, other audio and video media have shaped the narrative of this book. Created by Bradley Reeves, the Tennessee Archive of Moving Image and Sound (TAMIS) provided significant digital materials. In addition to Reeves's vast knowledge of Walker's public appearances, Eric Dawson guided me through the archival holdings at TAMIS. I extend my deepest appreciation to these contributors for providing the time and space to complete this project.

In addition to archives located in Knoxville, the "Archives of Appalachia" at East Tennessee State University in Johnson City also contain several videos of Cas Walker. Laura Elizabeth Smith guided me through several holdings, including film contributed by David West, Bradley Reeves, and Virgil Q. Wacks. Several of these have been uploaded to our Cas Walker website: http://caswalkerstories.utk.edu.

Not to be forgotten, the staff at the University of Tennessee Press has supported this project from its inception. As the acquisitions editor, Thomas

Wells has provided me much needed clarity regarding the publication process. Wells has always been supportive and his leadership, along with Scot Danforth's, has shepherded this project toward publication.

Others have offered their time and support to me throughout this process. To them—Elizabeth Eubanks, Max Matherne, Brittany Poe, Bradley Phillis, and Laura Roesch—I am forever grateful. And, finally, my wonderful wife Erica Spencer and our daughters Hazel and Harper have inspired me to reimagine Cas Walker for generations to come. While I acknowledge their contributions, a word of thanks is nothing compared to their unflinching support.

Josh Hodge at the East Tennessee History Center
being interviewed by Georgiana Vines
for his research into Cas Walker.
Photo by Georgiana Vines.

EDITOR MEMORIAL
Joshua S. Hodge (1984–2019)

Joshua S. Hodge received his BA from Auburn University, and his MA in history from the University of Alabama at Birmingham. As a doctoral student at the University of Tennessee, he concentrated on southern and environmental history. He won a number of the department's research and teaching awards, as well as several external fellowships, and was a valued member of the UT History Department's community. He received his PhD in May 2019, completing a dissertation entitled, "Alabama's Public Wilderness: Reconstruction Politics, Natural Resources, and the End of the Southern Commons, 1866–1905."

In the summer that Josh began research on his dissertation, as well as this oral history of Cas Walker, he was diagnosed with glioblastoma, an aggressive brain cancer. He died on May 23, 2019. Through these years of good work and all the challenges of his illness, he was supported by his wife, Erica Spencer, and his daughter, Hazel, to whom this book is dedicated.

INTRODUCTION

Cas Walker, Knoxville, and the American Century

In the spring of 1902, Orton Caswell "Cas" Walker was born near "the Sinks" in Sevier County, in the hills of East Tennessee. Born to Thomas Walker and Annie Stephens Walker, Cas was the seventh of twelve children. Growing up, he heard tales from his father about fighting as a member of the "blue bills," a vigilante group that battled the "white caps" who had terrorized the region in the post–Civil War years. In his early teens, Cas volunteered for the United States Navy. Though he was too young to serve, navy doctors fixed his wandering eye. When he returned home, Cas devoted himself to a variety of hard jobs, working to help support his family. He crossed the Great Smoky Mountains to shovel coal in North Carolina. Sometime between his first appearance in the coal camps and his arrival in Knoxville, Cas ventured to the Plains states where he baled and loaded hay. Returning to coal camps in Brookside and Ages, Kentucky, he clerked in company stores and "carried water" for card players. Whether hauling coal or peddling wares, Cas hustled. He staged "chicken shoots" in which each participant paid a nickel per shot—a precursor to a publicity stunt he used years later in his Knoxville grocery stores, throwing chickens off the roof to attract customers.

Moving to Knoxville in 1924, Walker opened his first store at 1100 East Vine Avenue with money he had saved from his early entrepreneurship. He delivered groceries to local customers, towing the wagon himself, and began to learn how to win the loyal "trade" of his Knoxville neighbors.

From his country upbringing, Walker rose to build a grocery empire. By 1932, at only thirty years of age, he had ten grocery stores. Though the Great Depression slowed the pace of Walker's expanding cash stores, at the height of his entrepreneurial career he owned at least twenty-seven retail ventures. These could be found in Knoxville—on Western Avenue, Magnolia Avenue, or in Happy Holler, to name a few—but he also founded grocery stores in

Appalachia and Pennington Gap, Virginia, and in eastern Kentucky as well. Even as his fortune grew, Cas retained and even cultivated his country-boy image, wearing rumpled suits, calling himself "the ole coon hunter," promoting the region's many great bluegrass and country musicians, and publishing weekly columns that often reminisced about his adventures growing up in the mountains of East Tennessee.

In 1928 Cas married Virginia Grantham, a childhood sweetheart, and sired a daughter, Wilma June, in 1930. Though he and "Ginnie" had only one child, they took in other family members, including a nephew, Odell Cas Lane, who eventually became a state representative and one of Walker's political allies.

In the mid-twentieth century Cas served two abbreviated terms as mayor, while serving for some thirty years as a city councilman. Voters first elected Cas to the city council in 1941. The first mayoral term came in 1945, but he was recalled overwhelmingly on December 3, 1946. Later, he served as "acting mayor" in 1959 after the death of Mayor Jack Dance. Though Cas's final term on the city council ended in 1971, he spent nearly another decade in local politics while serving on the Knox County Housing Authority. There he attended meetings, decided the location of public housing, and caused a ruckus when he abruptly fired one of his political rivals, "Cadillac Jack" Cooper. Perhaps Cas's final act in politics involved his work to help elect Knoxville's youngest mayor, Randy Tyree, and the subsequent fight over the 1982 World's Fair. Throughout his political career, Cas's reputation as a "bare-knuckle" politician meant that anyone who opposed him would have to put up a fight—at least once, quite literally.

Outside of politics, Walker became a legend for his role in showcasing local talent on his radio and television shows. He began as a public announcer in the late 1940s and early 1950s for country and gospel radio programs. His first television show appeared in the evening on WATE in 1956. The WBIR station, which aired his popular morning show—Cas Walker's "Farm and Home Hour"—did not exist until later that year. The morning show hosted Dolly Parton's first television appearance when she was only in high school, but she had already performed on Cas's radio program in Knoxville at age ten. Dolly and Cas sustained a friendship until his death in 1998, and Cas can be credited with nurturing the careers of many excellent musicians. But he did not always recognize quality talent on his show. His firing of the young Everly Brothers is a case in point. Nevertheless, through the years viewers watched some of East Tennessee's phenomenal entertainers, alongside a string of amateur cloggers and gospel singers. Rock and rollers like the band "Poker" tried their set on Walker's show, too, only to be shuffled offstage by Cas in a huff.

Cas displayed his entrepreneurial talent in his grocery-store chain, his gruff charisma on radio and television, and his political prowess in city hall. While these were major elements of Walker's career, he also dabbled in other areas. He produced the *Watchdog* newspaper, in which he lambasted political opponents with nicknames and folksy ridicule. He bought, trained, and sold prize-winning show horses and hunting dogs, using the latter to track raccoons in upcountry Georgia. Though his political fortunes began to wane in the 1980s, he continued his "against it"—or, as he would say, "agin' it"—attitude until his last days. Cas died in the fall of 1998 and, in the end, left an indelible impression on the city of Knoxville. The legend of his life that has persisted into the twenty-first century—as told by local Knoxvillians—is the subject of this book.

When I moved to the city in 2013 to join the doctoral program in history at the University of Tennessee, I had never heard of Cas Walker. As an out-of-towner ignorant of local politics, much less local folklore, I had overlooked the traces of Cas Walker still draped over the city. His picture hangs at the Time Warp Tea Room in Happy Holler. At Ciderville Music in Powell, David West and an assortment of talented pickers still sit and reminisce about the legend of the "Ole Coon Hunter." Former politicians such as Jack Sharp, Robert Booker, and Randy Tyree still mention the man with whom they had no choice but to engage in their own political careers.

With praise came scorn, however. Many younger and more cosmopolitan Knoxvillians found Walker's outlandish antics and bumpkin image an embarrassment. But even many of his critics came to grudgingly admire the grocer's knack for marketing ploys. Whether scattering freshly ground JFG Coffee beans along his store floors to stimulate sales, attracting crowds by throwing chickens off the roof, or luring customers by burying a man in the parking lot of his Chapman Highway grocery store, Cas Walker knew how to command everyone's attention. Who could forget the photo of Walker attempting to punch a fellow councilman that was published in *Life* magazine and distributed globally? Indeed, this conflict with J. S. Cooper showed the outside world just how "scruffy" the city could be. He believed there was no such thing as bad publicity, as long as they said, or spelled, his name right.

Any Knoxvillian born before 1980 remembers the gravelly voiced grocer-millionaire. Nearly twenty years since his death, stories of Walker's marketing antics and dominating personality retain an important place in the city's collective memory. He is the hero, the underdog, the truth-teller, and often the joker of the city's urban folklore. He stayed in the public eye for much of his life—through radio, television, and newspapers—which spanned most of the twentieth century. From "coon-dog" peddler to marketing mastermind, from his fight against fluoridation of the city's water to his manipulation of local elections, Cas spoke his mind—and in colorful ways that many still remember.

This book brings together the recollections of various Knoxvillians who agreed to share their own Cas Walker stories in long-form interviews. These are supplemented with stories submitted by many in the region who never met the man but certainly knew his legend. Our interviewees consist of many Knoxville notables, including former mayors and councilmen, political opponents, civil rights activists, historians, and musicians. Written submissions contain stories ranging from newcomers' first impressions of East Tennessee through Cas's television programs to awkward job-interview experiences at his Tennessee Valley Advertising Agency and, of course, Dolly's first television appearance. The collected stories include much truth, but they also contain a dose of mythology. I hope that they help capture the cultural richness surrounding the many memories of Cas Walker that reveal so much about twentieth-century Knoxville. Yet, to strike a balance between fact and fiction, I have also scoured Cas Walker's biographical clippings files, his *Watchdog* newspaper, and other archival materials held at the Calvin M. McClung Collection at the East Tennessee History Center (ETHC). By melding together previously published materials with recent recollections of this millionaire man of the people, this book gathers a rich set of resources for the people of Knoxville and the students of its history.

I was invited to join this project by my advisor and UT history professor Ernest Freeberg. When Freeberg arrived in Knoxville, he happened to purchase a quaint home on Gaston Avenue, the house in North Hills in which Walker had lived for most of his life. Multiple visitors came by, eager to tell some of their Cas Walker stories. As the sale proceeded, he found stacks of paperwork and knick-knacks in the basement of the home and, as a proper historian, thought that a local museum or archive would surely want this cache of primary resources produced by Cas. By the time the sale had finalized, Freeberg returned to find that all the items had vanished into thin air. While those relics of the past have yet to be found, members of the

Knoxville community, Freeberg thought, would still remember Walker as his pronounced presence had been burned into their memories.

In the pages that follow, the reader will find new and old materials that consider key moments in the twentieth century: the Great Depression, the "red scare" era, and the civil rights movement, to name a few. While these vignettes from Walker's life do not offer an exhaustive examination of each subject, one does gain a sense of how regional, national, and global events affected Knoxville. Through his sustained relationship with local television and newspaper media, Walker commented frequently on essentially every topic the city council or mayor's office tackled. Known for being "agin' it," Walker earned a reputation among many for standing against progress and holding the city back. Some even claim that Knoxville would be only a little country town if it had been left up to Cas Walker. But, as this book shows, Walker served as an important balance, if a negative one, to the newest trends in local government and the progressive ideas that he so often viewed with suspicion.

Walker was a walking contradiction, and this may be one reason why his story continues to fascinate so many. He was a millionaire who intentionally dressed down so that the less affluent could identify with him. He sent flowers to funeral homes and provided burial money for the needy but simultaneously reinforced his reputation as a bare-knuckle politician and entrepreneur by threatening to "whoop" any potential robbers. Love him or hate him, Cas Walker's shadow continues to shape perceptions of Knoxville's past and visions of its future. One can only hope, as I do, that the legend of Cas Walker is memorialized in this book for Knoxville's benefit as a new century without him has dawned.

The following chapters contain transcribed oral history stories, previously published newspaper articles, and written submissions. In an effort to capture the genuine voices that make up this book, I have chosen to publish the stories as close to their original forms as possible. As he said about his own editorials—and as is mirrored in this book—Cas Walker stories are "supposed to have mistakes."

Introduction 5

"Cas Walker Family." Ca. 1910s. Cas stands second from the left in the back row. Printed by permission of the McClung Collection, East Tennessee History Center.

CHAPTER 1

"I Never Did Try to Act Better Than Anybody"

Scenes from Cas Walker's Early Life

Nobody enjoyed telling a good Cas Walker story more than Cas Walker himself. In his weekly "Cas Says" newspaper columns and in his autobiography, *My Life History*, he loved to tell tales about his rough-and-tumble childhood in the mountains of East Tennessee. While Cas played an integral role in shaping his public persona, the people of Knoxville—customers, voters, and listeners—perpetuated many of the stories about Cas's early life. In this chapter, Betty Bean's *Metro Pulse* article describes Cas's entry into Knoxville. Other recollections—from historian Bruce Wheeler and Walker himself—reveal the man's frugality and work ethic. These characteristics catapulted Walker from the coal camps of the mountains into the big city and established him as a notable member of the business community.

"Pure Horatio Alger"

★ *Metro Pulse*, July 30, 1998, by Betty Bean (Excerpt)

Cas Walker's life story is pure Horatio Alger. He was born March 22, 1902, to Tom and Annie Stephens Walker, who worked a hardscrabble Sevier County farm near the Sinks. There were 12 children, and Cas counted himself "the youngest, the meanest and the prettiest" of the boys.

His young life was greatly influenced by his father's membership in a group called the Blue Bills, which had been formed to combat the White Caps, a band of masked vigilantes who marauded around Sevier County during the last decade of the 19th Century. Its reign of terror ended with a double hanging on the courthouse lawn in 1899.

In the [book] *White Caps and the Blue Bills of Sevier County*, which Cas Walker published in 1974, he says, "All during my school years in going to and from school, I lived in constant threat and my brothers and sisters did likewise because my father was a Blue Bill and helped to hang Catlett Tipton and Pleas Wynn who were White Caps." Maybe that was one of the reasons Walker left home early and often. He walked across the mountain when he was 14 to work in a Champion Fiber and Lumber Company logging camp in Smokemont, N.C., with the aim of making enough money to pay off the mortgage on the family farm, which was threatened with foreclosure. He also put back tuition money so he could attend Murphy College, a Sevierville secondary school where he waited tables and did janitorial work to earn his keep. There, he was tormented by the more affluent city kids for his rough clothes and country manners.

Fed up with his snooty classmates, he ditched school in 1919 and headed for Kansas, where he worked on a ranch and then hoboed around the West. Then he was on to the coal camps of Kentucky, where he brawled his way into his twenties and, by 1923, had made enough money digging coal to save $850, which he used to buy himself a grocery store in Knoxville.

His mining experience, Walker said, "Made me feel like I'd skinned the world and gutted it, too." Armed with this confidence, the brash young Walker barged uninvited into Knoxville's business community. . . .

★ Cas Walker, *My Life History*

Murphy College

I never did try to act better than anybody, or pretend to have a great education. I was always just a good ole country boy and people liked me for being that way.

I did go to Murphy College in Sevierville for about two years and then I ran off to Kansas. At Murphy College I would work by waiting on tables to pay half of my tuition. I also janitored some by cleaning three library buildings and a big auditorium at the school.

I sorta hate to tell this next story, but I've always fought for right, and at times I've had to physically fight. I took wrestling in school, and I sure wasn't no push-over for anybody.

The boys who were raised in downtown Sevierville felt as if they were better than us mountain boys. One time a city boy tripped me and he did it on purpose! He sat down and made faces at me. He had caused me to fail my school lesson, and then he said he wanted to meet me outside after school. He had got my dander up! He said that he was going to beat my tail, but I knew that he'd have to bring his lunch.

When school was over, I hurried outside and gave him what he wanted. We had the darnest fist fight you ever saw! I whipped his tail good! He went home and got his brother and daddy and they all come back. While I was sweeping out the library building I found a baseball bat, I thought they might come back for me, so I had put the baseball bat where I could get to it. I'm glad I did! The old man asked me if I thought I could whip all three of them. I told him I was willing to try, and then I let that bat do the talking. They got in a couple of licks on me, but I beat the devil out of them!

There was a good christian [*sic*] lady who worked in the library and she started praying. With the help of the good Lord and a baseball bat, I got the victory.

First Store in Five Points

★ Bruce Wheeler

And so he collected a fair amount of money and then he came to Knoxville and opened this store. Now people, of course, associate it with Cas Walker grocery stores, but it wasn't a grocery store, it was a store that was down in the red-light district. And it sold things that the people living there might want. He actually told me once that men would come in with these ladies—and he had taken soap and he had a glass counter and he had covered that counter with soap—but he had little eyeholes so the women could look through it and they could pick out some underwear that they wanted, and then Walker would wrap it up and sell it.

★ Cas Walker, *My Life History*

A Finger for an Ear

Not long after I went into the grocery business, in fact, this was my first store, I kept a horse and a wagon to delivery my groceries. A man came

Sketch of Walker's first store at 1100 E. Vine Avenue. *Knoxville Journal.* No date provided.

into my store and asked me if I would move a stone for him with my horse and wagon. I said, "I sure will." He asked, "What will you charge me?" I answered, "It will cost you a dollar." Some of the boys in the store told me that he would not pay his debts. I said, "He will pay me or I will beat it out of him." I moved the stone for him. He promised to pay me the dollar on Friday and he didn't even speak to me. Then, I was coming home from the store on Sunday and I met him and he didn't speak to me again. I stopped him and told him, "I told you if you didn't pay me the dollar that I would beat it out of you." He said, "You can't." I tied into him and he was very much of a man. I was getting the best of him, when he grabbed my hand and bit my middle finger off at the first knuckle. Then I grabbed him by the ear and bit just about all of his ear off.

They took me to the hospital and I carried the end of [my] finger in the palm of my hand. The doctor fixed my finger and it is still crooked to this day.

This man beat me to the hospital and no one was in the room but him when I went in, after having my finger treated. I had about bit his upper lip off as well. He was babbling about something and I whipped him again in the treatment room. He rebit my finger off and the doctor [put] it back again. I went back to my aunt and uncle[']s house where I was boarding. The next morning I got up and went to work at my store on Vine Street.

This man never paid me the dollar but they never did stop shopping at my store. He died approximately two months later with pneumonia fever.

I went to the funeral home to view the body just to see how much ear I had chewed off. It was all gone except a small bit at the ear lobe.

I've got some advice I want to pass out to everybody. Don't ever try to beat a dollar out of anyone!

★ *Knoxville News-Sentinel,* April 19, 1961

"Cas Walker Says"

On April 17, 1924, I came to Knoxville as a coal digger from Brookside and Agee's, Kentucky. . . . I went into the grocery business at 1100 East Vine Avenue. I actually knew nothing about the grocery business, but being humble and just admitting to my customers that I really needed their help and just being frank with them and telling them how badly I needed their help, I think did more than anything to make my venture a success.

Of course, I was willing to work long hours. I was honest. I told my customers the truth. I treated them good and they treated me good....

My first delivery system to get my produce from the market was a big oversize red coaster goat wagon.... I took the part of the goat.

Later on, through the sympathy of a very kind old soul, who sold me a big type pony for fifty dollars and traded it out in groceries. Another good old soul, who was a blacksmith, Mr. Coleman, gave me a little grocery wagon and fixed it up for me.... Then I was really in business. I had something to go to the market with, something to deliver with, and this really put me on my way.

★ Bennie Wallen Jean

One of the things that he did that was really amazing is how he got his start in the grocery business. He worked in the coal mines up in Kentucky, I think seven or eight years, but he saved every penny. And I mean he would sleep out, do anything to save a dime. So he come to Knoxville, and he put every dime he had in that first grocery store on Vine Avenue, downtown.

Anyway, one of the things he did to get business was he got the former owner's record book where people paid cash or put it on credit. So, he took all those names and addresses and phone numbers, and he called 'em up—even if they had paid up, he called 'em up and said, "So-and-so says that you owe him so many dollars," and they'd claim they had paid him.

And Mr. Walker said, "Well, if you'll trade with me, I'm willing to forgive you of all your debts"—even if they were paid or not paid.

You know, they thought, "Well, what a great deal this is!" So they started, they came back trading with him.

★ *Knoxville News*, September 2, 1925

"Whipped Another's Boy"

Ed Cooper and Cas Walker were arrested by Officer Householder for fighting. The cause of it was a whipping Walker had given Cooper's little 8-year-old son. Cooper claimed Cas should have come to him instead of taking correction upon himself. He said: "Children are born into the world against their own will. People should have backing in correcting them; I try to raise my boy properly, and send him to Sunday school and daily school."

Walker was fined $10 for whipping the boy and $5 for fighting.

Cas Walker's grocery store in Bearden. Printed by permission of the *Knoxville News Sentinel*.

CHAPTER 2

"If I'd Thought of a Few More Things, I'd Have Stooped a Little Lower"

Selling Groceries

Cas Walker had a knack for selling groceries. His promotions—even his presence—attracted everyday shoppers. Over the course of the twentieth century, Cas delved into many areas of advertising, including signs, television commercials, and on-site contests. His marketing savvy, however, could not dispel rumors about the contents of his grocery stores. This chapter explores several elements of Cas's grocery empire: the outlay of his stores, the development of his own brands of products, and how he made the best out of an otherwise sour situation. Customers also describe their experiences shopping in a Cas Walker Grocery Store. The chapter ends on a "Flood Sale" in Pennington Gap, Virginia, Walker's marketing of Supraderm Salve, and his threats to "whoop" potential robbers.

"Particular Ideas about Groceries"

★ James Bragg

He had particular ideas about groceries. He wanted your produce first, because people bought produce on an impulse. You might not put that bunch of bananas or some pears or whatever [in your basket], if you know you're running out of money at the end: "Oh lord, I've already spent too much." He thought that was an impulse buy.

Then they had the canned goods and everything else, but you always had to have your milk toward the end, because you wanted it to stay cold when you go home. If you put it toward the front you might bypass it, or you might only go get that item and then leave.

Bread was always last, because you don't want to get your bead crushed, so it's on top. The bag boys would have to take care of it, set it aside, they had a little shelf on the side of the register that they put the bread there, then they'd load everything else. And that will go on top because they didn't want the bread smashed.

I've been into other stores with him as a kid. He'd say, "Let's go over to A&P."

He'd walk in and everybody said, "Hey, that's Cas Walker!"

If a new store came into town he would point out to me, "Well, this is what's wrong with this store, it shouldn't have that setup."

But Cas wanted his managers to be up front. They would kind of just oversee the show, but they would be up there at the cash register. And my dad, a lot of times he would carry out as many groceries as the bag boy. They would pay him to do it, because that's what brought people back—being friendly.

When he was in his own business he said, "I can pay somebody to put stock up. I can do my bookwork after hours or at home or pay a CPA to do it. I'm going to be out here selling groceries." And that had to be from Cas.

Now where Cas got it, I don't know.

A Sprinkle of Blue Band Coffee

★ Larry Mathis

In his old days, when he first had one or two stores, they had sawdust floors in them. In the early '40s, wartime, people didn't care what a store was as long as it had whatever they needed to go in there and get. When the floors got dirty, they swept it out, put new sawdust down. That's what it was. Didn't have no vacuum cleaners and things like that then.

Cas ground his own coffee and what he would do, he would take and grind a pound of coffee every morning and he'd just go sprinkle it all through the floor in that sawdust. And when people come in that's the first thing they'd smell. They'd go right back there and get them a pound of coffee.

★ Carl Warner

Then he got upset with his butchers because when the meat came in to sell, they were trimming it, and when they trimmed the meat, very often, they weren't careful and they would not only trim the fat but they would trim some of the beef on there. And so he said, "What are you doing with this?"

They said, "We're throwing it out."

He said, "No, no, no, no!"

So, he had to package it in two-pound packaging and called it "family pack" and sold it for a pretty good price. And people would buy it because it was cheap, but at least he got money for it instead of having the butchers throw it out.

It was called "Cas Walker's Family Pack" and it was like, 80 cents or 60 cents a pound or whatever.

★ Bob Booker

Not only did I shop at the McCullough Avenue store, I lived in College Homes the whole time I was at Knoxville College, so I spent five years shopping at the Cas Walker Store that was on Western Avenue. I had my share of both of them. Then I shopped at the Magnolia Store which was also in the black community. So we had three stores that were in the black community.

[But] the food was not up to par. Cas Walker had some of the worst meat anybody could buy. And you tried to eat it, but I wasn't successful. One time I gave some to my dog, my dog wouldn't eat it. So that's terrible to say, but there was something wrong—I don't know if he took groceries out of other stores when it got to be, when it shouldn't be sold, and brought it to stores or not. I couldn't talk about that in a court of law, because I just don't know. But the food was suspect.

I think he compared well with what else was going on in terms of aesthetics and that kind of thing. I just don't think that his stuff was as fresh as other stores.

★ Bruce Wheeler

One of the problems, which never really came out so much in the open, is the prices were just a little bit higher than Kroger and White stores and things. Partly I think because of the insurance he might have had to buy for some of these stores, which is where they were placed.

But then there was a lot of off-brand products that were sold. There was a company that he owned that made soft drinks and applesauce and stuff. That stuff got sold in the stores, but you wouldn't see name brands.

I never ate any of it, I never shopped there. It just didn't look great, the lettuce and the whatever just looked a little bit old.

★ Ben Walker

You know everybody in Knoxville talked about how nasty his stores were. They were kinda dirty for me too, but everything's nasty now.... But they'd talk about how nasty his store was, and his meat department. I didn't see it. I worked for him and I did not see anything. I'm a clean person and I did not see that.

And I know that some of the big restaurants in Knoxville, they bought all their meat from Cas Walker. They would come and buy hundreds of pounds of meat and sell it in the restaurant. One of my good friends was one of his butchers. I remember they would bring half of a cow—it'd take a big man to carry half of a cow—from Swift Food. These meat packing companies, they'd deliver half of cows, they'd cut em up right there in the store. I never saw anything like that.

Like I said, these people who talk about him selling bad meat, they don't know that the restaurants were buying meat from Cas and serving it for a big price!

Some of his stores did not smell too good, I will admit.

"Stop at the Sign of the Shears"

★ Bo Pierce

His main slogan was "Stop at the Sign of the Shears" and the name Cas Walker. They were like scissors, but it was old-fashioned, big shears, they used to call them. He wore tie tacks that were open shears, just like his logo on his stores. I don't know when Kroger started and I don't know where they started, but I was told that he got [a] considerable amount of money out of Kroger when they started the cost-cutter—again I can't remember if that was in the '60s or '70s. Kroger's slogan as they started growing was "cost-cutter," but they were using scissors, shears. Cas, he may have gotten stock even back then, in trade for using his shears.

★ Cas Walker, *My Life History*

The Sign of the Shears

I had a friend who was a sign maker, he made all kinds of signs. He told me that he could make me a deal on a sign that I could put in from of my store that would draw more people.

I said, "I've always thought about a Sign of the Shears a cutting a dollar in two." He told me that he would do it, and it would get me more attention than anything I could think of.

That was probably one of the greatest promotional ideas I had. Today I wear a tie pin with the "Sign of the Shears."

Kroger has star[t]ed using the shears, but their shears clips straight down and mine clips across.

★ Bill Routh

My brother, Greg, remembers a time when Dad was running errands and went by the office Cas maintained in the store on Central Avenue, in Happy Holler. (Later he moved this office to Chapman Highway, where a traffic light was installed for his convenience.) When Cas walked out with Dad to the car, he saw Greg sitting there and asked if Greg ever wore a tie. Dad replied, "Yes, to church." Cas went back into his office and came out with a tie bar containing the "Sign of the Shears." As far as I know, Greg may still have that memento.

Billboards and Other Kinds of "Hype"

★ Bob Booker

Along with the success, there was even more hype. Hype means you can be failing to the max, but if you can prove that you're successful in hype, that counts for something.

And Cas was a master at all of it. "We may doze, but our stores never close." "Shop at the sign of the Shears where we're constantly cutting prices." Slogans similar to that—I mean, the guy was a genius at that.

★ Bruce Wheeler

There was a big billboard as you went out of town on I-40, and it said—there's a picture of it somewhere: "The three greatest things in the world: possum, watermelon, and Cas Walker."

I thought, "Sweet Jesus."

★ Ernie Gannon

One of our sales people sold [Cas Walker] sixteen billboards in the summer of 1972. He bought a truckload of watermelons for each of his stores. On the billboard it had across the top: "What's better than . . ." with a big picture of a raccoon on the left hand side and a big watermelon on the right hand side. Across the bottom it had: "Cas Walker Supermarkets."

One morning, he got to work early and the phone rang and it was Cas. "This is Cas Walker," he said.

"You know that billboard you got on Kingston Pike next to my store in Bearden?—Somebody's climbed up on that billboard and wrote 'pussy.'"

We told him that we'd fix it and Cas said, "No, that's good advertising."

We waited until about noon to go down and cover it up, as the billboard company didn't want to catch any flak. Later, Cas remembered that campaign and they sold a lot of watermelons!

★ James Bragg

J. Bazzel Mull was a great friend of Cas. He lived to be ancient. And he actually preached at Cas's funeral. He was Cas's age, maybe—they were best buddies.

It's really kinda neat to hear a TV preacher talking to [his] best friend: "Dammit, J. Bazzel!" and they'd get into it. "Cas, that's a bunch of shit! That don't make any sense." To me, to hear that, it was funny. I thought, "I can't believe a preacher said that." They were great friends, and I don't know how far that went, if it's just from being neighbors or whatever.

But J. Bazzel's blind, he could barely see, all he could see was light, I think. So, on his show—now Cas may have bankrolled that, I don't know, 'cause he sold Cas Walker groceries—but J. Bazzel would sit there with his wife, Mrs. Mull, and a little girl, Charlotte, and every Sunday, for an hour, they would have gospel music. They'd have different groups on there and they would sing gospel music. Then he would make some comments and sell some groceries for Cas.

I remember one day, he says—and I don't know if you've heard the deal that Cas said that they've got the biggest nuts in town and his meat can't be beat, have you heard that one? That happened.

Well, actually, J. Bazzel's the one that got that going, per my dad. He said that J. Bazzel was on TV, and he says, it was around Christmastime, and he's selling some groceries, and he says, "Cas Walker's got the biggest nuts in town, ain't that right, Mrs. Mull?"

Everything he said, it was, "Ain't that right, Mrs. Mull?"

"That's right, J. Bazzel."

And he's the one that said that. And Cas thought it was so funny that he gets on his TV show and says, "We've got the biggest nuts in town, and our meat can't be beat." And I don't know if he meant . . .

My dad's thinking, "Oh lord." And my Aunt Ginnie's mortified that he would say something like that. He thought it was funny. He loved it, 'cause everybody's talking about it!

But that happened. It's a true story. But J. Bazzel is the one that actually started it.

★ Cas Walker, *My Life History*

30 Days of Unexpected Excitement

When I opened my store on Clinton Highway, it was the first store that I had that stayed open all day and all night. The reason that we stayed opened day and night was because we couldn't lock it up. It didn't have any front doors. My carpenters had been so busy working on other things to get the store ready to open that they didn't have time to open the store like I'd told everybody I would, we just went ahead and opened the store without any doors and kept it opened day and night.

To promote the grand opening, I'd gotten a five hundred pound helium balloon to fly over the store during the daytime. We'd take it down at night and put it back up the next morning. I had to have three men there to put it up in the air every morning. One morning two of them didn't show up. This other fella, that kinda always wanted to do things on his own anyway, went ahead and put the air in the balloon, cut it loose, and grabbed the rope himself. Of course it took him straight up in the air. It went around and around the top of the building and finally he fell on the roof of the store. Now I bet that balloon stirred around this part of the country for a month. Everybody around here was walking around looking up. You talk about something that caused excitement that balloon floating around caused excitement.

That balloon went all the way to Middlesboro Kentucky and all over around Pineville, Kentucky, and back to Knoxville. It floated around for about a month before it finally landed down near a river below Chattanooga. People came from up in Kentucky and all around to buy groceries at a store that we didn't have time to close.

I also had a great big sign on the top of the building that went from one end of the building to the other. The sign had my picture on it along with a picture of a possum and a picture of a watermelon. The sign said, "The three greatest things in the world, —Cas Walker, a possum, and a watermelon." That got lots of attention but it didn't get as much attention as that five hundred pound balloon floating loose all over the country. I never had used a balloon before, but I don't guess I ever used anything that got as much attention as that did.

I've done a lot of funny things but that got more attention than anything else I ever did. That store turned out to be one of my greatest stores.

★ James Bragg

Cas would do strange things. I remember one time that he had a TV show—it was like a ten-minute thing that came on every night during the week—and it was a horserace.

He was passing these tickets out, coupons, and when you bought a bag of groceries, you got a coupon. So you'd rush home and you'd watch this ten-minute add-on at the end of the Early Show. There used to be a show that came on TV, the Early Show, it'd be like an hour-and-a-half movie, and there'd be commercials all the way through it. Then, at the end of it, Cas Walker would have his horserace. It wasn't live, it was like a taped thing.

Maybe a horserace from who knows where—and it might have been three years ago, but you'd get these cards and if you won, then you got a decent prize, fifty dollars maybe, or whatever.

There'd probably only be like two or three winners in the whole Cas Walker system, but everybody'd watch it. That was one of his schemes.

Marketing Margarine and "Watering" the Competition

★ Bob Lutrell

As far as Cas goes, he was a man that wanted to project himself. Either a good form or a bad form—it doesn't make any difference what they said as long as they were talking about him, that was his philosophy. He said, "I don't care what they say as long as they keep talking about me."

The first story I'll tell you about was this margarine Cas had that was called "Sunny Land." It was a generic brand you could buy in a box, the margarine, you could get it from any wholesaler. They'd put it in that Sunny Land book or carton.

He came up there to the paper one day, and he asked our artist if he would help him design a new carton. Woody said, "I'm too busy. Take it out there, Bob does freelance artwork and stuff like that." He came out there to my desk, and he said that he had an idea of what he wanted. He said, "I want this margarine to be more personal. I want it to be my margarine."

I said, "OK, Cas, what have you got in mind?"

He says "this is what I want"—and he started talking. He didn't have a sketch, he didn't have any drawings, he just talked. I was making some notes as he was talking and he said, "I want this boy to be a country boy. I want him sitting on a bank up against a tree with a fishing pole in his hand in the creek."

He says—this is how detailed he was—"I want freckles on the boy. I want a straw hat that's torn. I want blue jeans with a patch on his blue jeans. And I want him barefooted with a bandage around his toe."

I said, "Oh boy. What color blue jeans you want?"

He says, "Blue!" He said, "I want a dog sitting beside him, looking up at a limb on a tree. On that limb, I want a coon. I want that coon looking down at that dog." The fact that he was a coon hunter, he had to have that coon in there.

I said, "Yes sir, got you. Anything else?"

"No," he says, "you might put a bucket of worms by him."

It was natural for a boy to be fishing with a dog, and the way he described the way that boy oughta look was just something else, because you could just see those wheels turning in his head. His trade was country—he didn't go for the Kingston Pike, so to speak, West Knoxville crowd. He was the poor man's choice.

I said, "OK, we'll do that." I made a lot of notes and some sketches and stuff.

He left and I said, "I'll call you in about a day or two and let you look at a sketch that I've come up with."

So, being eager to make an extra buck, I go to the store and pick up a carton of margarine, Sunny Land. And I take the margarine out of it and flatten out the carton and put the ingredients on different flaps and so forth and so on, and put his title up there, "Cas Walker's Sunny Boy Margarine." That's what he wanted.

So I got it all sketched up. I called him up and told him, "Come up here and see if it's what you want."

He looked at it and said, "Yep, that looks good."

He says, "How much do I owe you?"

I said, "Aw, give me $75."

He wrote me a check right there. Next thing I knew, he had it on his television program—"Sunny Boy Margarine, the best in the land, no doubt about it."

Later on, he came down to the paper, and he says, "Man I have sold a ton of that thing. I sell about a carload a week. You should've took commission off of that!"

I said, "Who's gonna keep score, Cas?"

I took that $75 and bought me a new suit of clothes. I looked at the clothes the other day going through Dillard's down west in the mall, and they had suits down there on sale, $365, regular $595, a suit of clothes! I said, "No wonder everybody wears blue jeans!"

Even the preacher, they don't dress up in fine clothes anymore like that. Golly molly, shirts, $125!

★ Cas Walker, *My Life History*

High Water Advertising

One time there was a man who opened a store right down from my store. He put his produce out front like I did mine. I always thought mine was better because I kept it wet and looking good, and it would almost always talk to you.

Well, anyway, we were in competition, I had this employee of mine go down and spray some strong dog scent spray by this man's produce. Then she took a big old German Shepherd dog by there "accidentally" for a walk. When a dog smells dog scent they just automatically have to relieve themselves of water. Sure enough, when that big old shepherd smelled that scent he cocked his big old back leg, and brother, the water streamed!

I had another employee across the street with a camera and a zoom lens, and of course I got a picture.

The next day or two we both had purchased a page ad in the paper. His was pretty good, but my page had a picture of my produce, and of course a picture of his. His had a German Shepherd dog watering his!! He moved his produce indoors.

What do people mean when they say Cas Walker was a colorful character?!?

Life has been good and fun too! Of course, Cas Walker's produce was above the high water mark!

"About the Chickens"

★ Bob Lutrell

This brings me to a story that he had about the chickens. Somebody told him a joke about a three-legged chicken and I think he got the idea from that.

He said, "This guy was driving down the highway with his wife and looked out the side window.

There was a three-legged chicken running along beside them, looked like he was doin' 50 MPH."

He thought, "That's unusual." So he hit the gas a little bit and ran it up to 60 and that ol' chicken just kept right on running with him. He said, "Let me do 70." He did 70 and that ol' chicken *"whoosh"* right in front of him, ran over to a barnyard.

He pulled in right behind him and asked the old farmer, "Let me ask you something, have you got three-legged chickens in here?"

He says, "Yeah, I do."

"Well, how do they taste?"

He says, "I don't know. I never have caught one of them!"

I think that gave Cas an idea about a three-legged chicken. He gets the cut-up chickens, cut-up fryers, and he throws an extra leg in there, a drumstick.

So, he's going to be smart, he gets out and advertises, "three-legged chickens for sale"—same price as two-legged chicken, but these are three-legged. He promoted that and he sold them.

★ Cas Walker, *My Life History*

Throwing Chickens Off the Roof

When I first opened my store on Vine Avenue, I remember I only made twenty-seven dollars on my first Saturday. I knew that I needed a crowd, so I decided to get some frying chickens and throw them off the roof. It drew a crowd, and I threw fifty chickens off. People went wild! They were chasing chickens all over the parking lot! The chickens were squawling, children were screaming, and people were laughing, it was total confusion! It was great! That Saturday I made over twelve hundred dollars.

After the first crowd had disappeared, we had a "goose eating contest." We would see who could guess how many grains of corn a goose could eat. While this was going on, I sold peanuts, salted popcorn, and drinks. The salty popcorn made people thirsty, and I made my money on the drinks they bought. To top the evening off, we would have a "greasy pig" contest. I got about one hundred feet of wire and made a pen. I had a small pig and I greased it over with Vaseline. I had about six young boys that I put in the pen to catch the pig. I offered twenty-five dollars as a prize to anyone who could catch the pig. Of course, they could catch it, but they couldn't hold it. It was a sight to see! That caused a big crowd to assemble there at night. They would buy their groceries after these events.

★ James Bragg

Have you heard about the chickens coming off of the roof? Well, that's way before my time. My dad worked for Cas. He was a manager of one of his stores. He was manager on Broadway and over on Main Street, which has been demolished. It was in a poor section of town. My dad had been there so long that he remembered the chicken deal.

On Saturday mornings, I believe it was, he would get up on top of his grocery store, and he would throw chickens off. And while the crowd was there to get 'em a free chicken—I'm talking a live chicken!—then he would sell them some groceries. And that's a true story.

★ Cas Walker, *My Life History*

Baby Chickens

Here is something else that went over real big.

At Easter time, everybody would give away a chicken with a ten dollar grocery order. They would give folks a baby chick free. The children went for it just unbelievable, they would go for that!

One year I got my baby chicks five days old, and I didn't have but one out of the two hundred and fifty that died. I started to make my pitch on television (I had a television program in the mornings) and I was just making a big pitch how big and stout and healthy the baby chicks were, that I had. Everybody at home knew what big, sturdy, stout chickens I had! I was showing one on TV and the chicken fell deader than a door knob! I just couldn't hardly think about it. I said, "I have seen women fall or faint, but I ain't never seen no chicken fall dead." Everybody got a big kick out of that because of how much it embarrassed me. I was giving two of those chickens with a twenty-five dollar order free. It went over real big, but people still laughed about that.

They see me out sometimes, and they will call that to my attention. That was an embarrassing moment.

"Dullin' Spray"

★ Larry Mathis

I'll tell you a few little ol' funny stories. Out at Channel 10—and this was back before color TV—the studio had a kitchen in it, and they would fry Wampler sausage and had an ol' boy that was promoting White Lily Flower, and he'd come out and make biscuits sometimes and they'd fry sausage and we'd just eat sausage and biscuits every morning.

But they had this kitchen there, and of course, the great big thousand-watt bulbs that they used on the big studio lights, maybe two-foot across. And the lights were so bright, they would just burn you nearly, because it's so hot.

But anyhow, when the cameras would go in to shoot a real close-up of say, Wampler Sausage in a skillet, well, the skillet was stainless steel, and whenever the lights from the camera and the studio come in on that stainless steel, it would just turn black from the glare; you couldn't see anything.

They had a can of dullin' spray that made a matte finish on something, to cut the glare so you could actually see the sausage in the pan.

Cas had a little old grocery shelf that was sitting over there, a prop, with milk jugs and things like that.

One of the prop men there at Channel 10 accidentally set this can of dullin' spray over on Cas's grocery shelf. So, he got up that morning, he said, "We got Lux #303 size beans, three for 89 cents; we got JFG Coffee, 79 cents a pound; we got Kearns Bread, 29 cents a loaf; we got, uh,—*dullin' spray?!* I don't know what in the devil that is, but we bought a whole carload of it!" and just set it down and went on.

Of course, we just died laughing. We knew what it was.

★ Louie Chester Finley

My cousin worked for a local TV Station, I believe WATE or WBIR as an intern set director. He was setting up store shelves and products for a Cas Walker Store commercial, which was live in these days. Well, when Cas came out to promote his sales, he was working his way down the items, can tomatoes, green beans, boxes of cereal, & coffee, etc. He was saying we have this for $$, this $$ on a can of coffee, always saying they had a whole truck loads of these Cost Cutting Prices (his logo), and then all of a sudden he picked up a can of non-glare spray that my cousin had forgot and left on the shelves during set up. Cas looked at the can and didn't miss a lick, and said we just got a special truck load shipment of this in at $.99 a can.

"The Government Made Us Stop It"

★ Bennie Wallen Jean

One of the promotions Mr. Walker liked to do—he had to quit it because of political correctness—but one of the promotions he liked to do was have a pancake breakfast on the parking lot. It was free, and we had a lady that—I think she worked at city hall—she was a black lady and she looked exactly like Aunt Jemima. She dressed up like her and she would be there serving pancakes. Aunt Jemima furnished the pancake mix.

I went to one because I wanted to, I thought it was a funny thing to do. But they made us quit that because it was derogatory to the colored people. That woman was so mad because we paid her for doing that. See, that made her lose money. She told me she was just really mad about it, and I told her, "We are too." But the government made us stop it.

And then another thing he did that they made us quit was—this little colored boy we hired for advertising watermelons. We had that little song: [*singing*] "Cas Walker's melons are thumpin' good, thumpin' good, thumpin' good."

To this day, I know how to pick out watermelons. You look at a watermelon and if they're kinda yellow on the bottom, if they've been on the ground long enough to be good and ripe, and then if you flick them, if they sound like a low bass they're good—if they're high, they're green and don't have much juice. I've got one in my fridge now. When I go to pick it out, I do it and I say, "Well, this one's thumpin' good, I think!"

Anyway, they made us take that off the air, it was offensive. And the boy was making money. I think every time it ran, he got five dollars.

You know, over this political correctness—a lot of people get hurt by it. He liked doing it, and we made a film, we ran the film, every time it played, he got five dollars—I think it was five dollars.

Flood Sale and a $500 Mistake

★ Bennie Wallen Jean

Pennington Gap, Virginia. It flooded out and it ruined a lot of merchandise in there. But Mr. Walker told me if somebody handed you a lemon to make lemonade out of it. And so he goes up there and has a big flood sale, and he asked me to go on Saturday to help out. And people were comin' from all over buyin' stuff. One lady wanted to buy my raincoat that I had hung on the coat rack! So I said, "I can't sell that, that's mine!"

But that's how popular the sale was. He was makin' so much money off the flood sale that he decided to buy some merchandise and wet it down. So he did that and sold it as "damaged merchandise." He'd wet it down, and he made money after money on that flood sale.

They were just flooding in there buying stuff.

★ Larry Mathis

Cas had stores all over the place at one time. He had them up in Kentucky, in Pennington Gap, Virginia, in Morristown and Sevierville. All these satellite stores that he had.

One time, he started selling dry goods, like overalls and pillowcases and towels, not luxuries but just staples that you had to have at the house. Well, Pennington Gap store, up in Virginia, was right on the creek. You'd go out the back of the store, and there's the creek there, a pretty good-sized creek.

One time, it flooded, and got up in there, got stuff wet. Now, Cas had these overalls and things like that in several of his stores. Claude Boone had a van, and Cas would pay him to go take them to different stores. That was kind of one thing that he had Claude doing.

Well, he got them people to come out of the mountains up there, and they were just grabbing them overalls and things like that. What Cas did, he called Claude, he said, "Claude, go to those other stores and bring the overalls up here."

Claude just took a vanload of overalls up there. And what they did, Cas just took a hose and kind of sprayed them down just a little, not soaking wet. And they unfolded them, they didn't want them folded. They came and took them all and piled them on a table.

Well, those people grabbed them things, they thought they were getting a deal-and-a-half on that flood sale. Cas was smart, he would do things like that.

★ David West

Pennington Gap was having a promotion. That's way up there in the mountains, coal country. On his show he said, "I want everybody at Pennington Gap, everybody that's ever dug coal with me, I want you there Saturday, we've got a photographer, he's gonna make an 8×10 picture of me and you individually, and I'm giving it to you. I'm gonna give it you. It cost a dollar apiece and I'm giving it to you."

That's an expensive picture back when you can buy a Coke for a nickel or a dime. Now that's back when money was money.

He told me, "In that coal camp that I worked in, there was only fifty people that worked in it. You know they ain't gonna be but fifteen to twenty of them show up."

But $15 to $20 was big for that guy back then.

Then he told me, "David, I went up there and there was five hundred people standing out in the parking lot. I almost fainted. It cost me five hundred and some odd dollars. I just gritted my teeth. I didn't remember who even worked with me in the coal camp. You can't tell somebody he didn't work with you! "All right just line up here. It's gonna take us a little while, we're gonna get these."

He said the store, it did double, triple. I want to use this illustration: if the store was taking in $500 a day, it got up to $2,500 a day.

They started trading at that store. His quote is: "That store took off like a house on fire. I asked the store manager, 'What is going on? This store is taking in more than those big stores.'"

He said, "Well, it ought to, Cas. Your picture's on everybody's mantle in this whole town! You're in five hundred households! Everybody's in there bragging on you!"

See, that's a $500 mistake turning into thousands!

"Supraderm Salve Is No Joke"

★ *Metro Pulse,* July 30, 1998, by Betty Bean (Excerpt)

> Any type of sore, it will heal you up in two or three days. It will cure skin cancer, too, but I don't tell people that. My God, there is so many things it can be good for. I am afraid they will start thinking it is good for everything. There was a preacher that said "You know, at my church, Mr. Walker, people ask me to pray for them and I put oil on them and pray for them. The Bible says that, you know."
> It would be good judgment to use Supraderm Salve.
>
> —Cas Walker

It was Howard Dalton's job to manage the Knoxville stores. He went to work for Walker in 1939. He and his son Stevie work for the old man still, packing up cartons of Supraderm Salve to fill orders from as far away as a man in British Columbia who puts it on his Eskimo dogs.

Walker discovered the salve when Ginny brought some back from a Nashville horse show intending to use it on their grandson's athlete's foot. At the time, Cas was suffering from something he, with uncharacteristic delicacy, called "a colon bowel condition," for which he'd been treated at Johns Hopkins, where he said he had been told it was fatal. His friends remember it as a bad case of hemorrhoids.

In *My Life History,* he says he went home early one day itching so bad he just couldn't stand it anymore. He found a jar of salve, applied it to the afflicted area, and "My Lordy, it wasn't a few minutes until I got complete relief."

Cas liked the way the salve worked so well that he ordered 20 cases. Then he liked the way it sold so well that he decided to buy the company and was quoted a price of $5,000. But the demand he created made the owners jack the price up to $100,000. He agreed, and said he made the money back in 90 days, in part because he advertised the salve in *Full Cry,* a coon-hunter's magazine.

Cas Walker says
SUPERDERM SALVE
is
NO JOKE
"It saved my life about 50 years ago"

Some people would try to make a joke about it, but thousands of men and women would have had cancer if it hadn't been for SUPERDERM SALVE.

50 years ago I was suffering from hemorrhoids and possible colon cancer, John[s] Hopkins Hospital sent me home to die. Mrs. Walker had bought SUPERDERM SALVE for an athlete's foot remedy, and I used it for my hemorrhoids. It cleared up my hemorrhoids in five (5) days.

Many times surgery and cancer can be avoided by using SUPERDERM SALVE when hemorrhoids first gets started.

Another thing SUPERDERM salve can be used for is arthritis. It has been proven for years, we didn't advertise it. In the old days it was just advertised as "GOOD FOR ANYTHING." Arthritis is a disease thousands of people worry with, but remember that arthritis is a bone disease. SUPERDERM salve will give you relief for awhile, then you can come back and use it again and it will give you relief again. Use SUPERDERM SALVE for arthritis pain in your hands or feet.

ALWAYS USE SUPERDERM SALVE
When athlete's foot flares and GET RELIEF

PICK UP YOUR SUPERDERM SALVE AT MANY PLACES
IN KNOXVILLE

★ Bob Lutrell

Another time, he was, it was when he was living up there on Gaston Avenue, and he was sick and had a caretaker with him around the clock. But he still had his mind. I stopped up there to see him, and we were talking and I think that's the time he had invented Supraderm Salve. It was supposed to take care of your muscle aches and whether it was hot or cold, it worked either way, didn't make no difference. He got up there with his crooked finger, and he'd point to it and he'd say, "This'd grow hair on a billiard ball!"

I was up there and before I left, I said, "I better get out of here, I've stayed too long." But he loved to talk and go down memory lane.

He said, "You got any of that salve?"

I said, "I don't believe I have, Cas. I don't have any of that."

He told his housekeeper, "Go in there and get Bob a can of that salve."

I said, "That looks pretty good, you sure this stuff works?"

He said, "I'll guarantee it or your money back. It's got a money-back guarantee on it!"

He said, "That'll be five dollars."

I said, "I didn't come here to buy salve, Cas. As a matter of fact, I don't even have any change on me, I've gotta go to the bank."

"Ah," he said, "just take it."

But that's the way he was—he'd give you something and say, "That'll be five dollars," or "that'll be ten dollars."

Speaking to UT Students

★ *Knoxville News-Sentinel,* February 19, 1971

"'People Want To Be Fooled': Weird Ad Methods Work, Walker Says" by Charla Sear

Councilman-grocer-advertiser Cas Walker has told a group of UT advertising students, professors and professional advertisers that his advertising methods may not necessarily be the right ones, but they work. Mr. Walker spoke to the group last night at the UT Communications Building as part of the school's issue in Advertising program. . . .

"You've had some of the greatest people on earth tell you the right way to do things," the councilman told the group. "I'm going to show you the way I did things that may not be the right way, but it worked.

"But that's what advertising is, anyway," he said. "Whatever works."

Enjoys 'Fighting'

The owner of 22 stores in Tennessee, Virginia and Kentucky, he told the students he's "got big people to fight" for business, "and, brother, I like to fight them for it." He now has 27 percent of the market in Knoxville, he said, with his closest competitor at 25 percent.

He also said his early experience as a coal miner helped. "It makes me feel I've skinned the world and gutted it, too. I didn't like mining, but I sure liked the money I got from it," Mr. Walker said.

Tells of Giveaways

The grocer said he started in the grocery business by giving away frying chickens as a promotion to get people into the store. "Someone said I was crazy, and maybe I was," he said, "but they wasn't giving away no frying chickens."

Another big moneymaker was a cuckoo clock promotion. He got the clocks from Germany at a cost of 72 cents each, he said, and sold them at 99 cents with a $5 order.

Improvised Plan Paid Off

The Cas Walker 30-day Plan, he said, was dreamed up during a live television commercial, which was about to end too soon, while the director was motioning frantically for him to draw out the commercial to fill the allotted time.

"I don't know what the 30-day plan was," he said, "but it picked business up $300,000 a week. That put me in high clover."

Another time, in order to sell coffee, he ground up 10 pounds and sprinkled it in some sawdust on the floor in the main area of a store. "When you smell coffee, you want coffee," he explained.

But the promotion that brought the biggest laugh, from both the audience and the councilman himself, was "Dog Dippin' Day" held at his Pennington Gap, VA, store. Advertising "the same dip Cas Walker dips his own coon dog in" he gave away a "free $2 dip" with each $10 order.

"We dipped 737 dogs in two days," he said. "Business picked up $20,000 that weekend."

"People want to be fooled," Mr. Walker continued, "and we're not lily-white."

"We sell the fool out of cowboy steaks. What are cowboy steaks? Nothing but good ground chuck, rolled and sliced, and sold for 98 cents a pound."

Spends $7000 Weekly

Mr. Walker said he spends around $7000 a week on advertising. His advertising department is staffed by three people, including himself. "The things I've told you, they're crazy, silly," he told the students, "but still, that's advertising.

"People said they wouldn't stoop to some of my promotions, but, brother if I'd thought of a few more things, I'd have stooped a little lower."

"Beat the Hell" out of Thieves and Shoplifters

★ Rowdy Cope

Mr. Walker wasn't scared of the devil himself. And don't think he wouldn't fight with you if you got down to it. He had several times at his stores that he'd have actually a fight.

Fact is, he told them way back yonder—people would leave his stores and people would rob customers outside. He told them on television, "I'm gonna be waitin' for you. And I'm gonna have people out there that when you start to do something like that, they're gonna beat the hell out of you!"

★ *People's Press,* September 8, 1994

"Cas Says..."

I'd like to mention again this week that shoplifting is a much bigger problem than most people realize. Because people steal so much stuff, it causes everybody to have to pay more for what they buy.

One time we had a man who started coming into one of my stores and just taking what he wanted and then just walking out. He brought his own market basket and shopped out my merchandise, and took it out the door without paying for it. Of course when I found out about it, I made it my business to be there to greet him personally.

Sure enough, he must of thought he was Cas Walker himself. He gathered up what he wanted and walked out the door with my goods. I followed him. When I told him to give me my merchandise, he pulled out a long hunting knife and said he was going to give me that instead. That was the last words that came out of his mouth before I shot him between the eyes with a Smith-Wesson thirty-two revolver.

For some reason, the bullet didn't penetrate his head. Instead it traveled around the skin of his skull and lodged. We commenced fighting and I beat him down the street for about a half a block with that pistol before the police got there. They took him off to jail and he made bond.

After the fight, I asked the policemen what they wanted me to do. They said, "Get you a bigger pistol."

While this man was out on bond, there was a fine old gentleman who opened a little market down the street from me. The kids were crazy about him. He was always giving them candy.

This thief went in that market and killed the poor old fellow. I had my morning TV show then and I dubbed him the "Santa Claus Killer." That got on the news and it spread like a fire across dry wheat.

He was captured and sent to the electric chair.

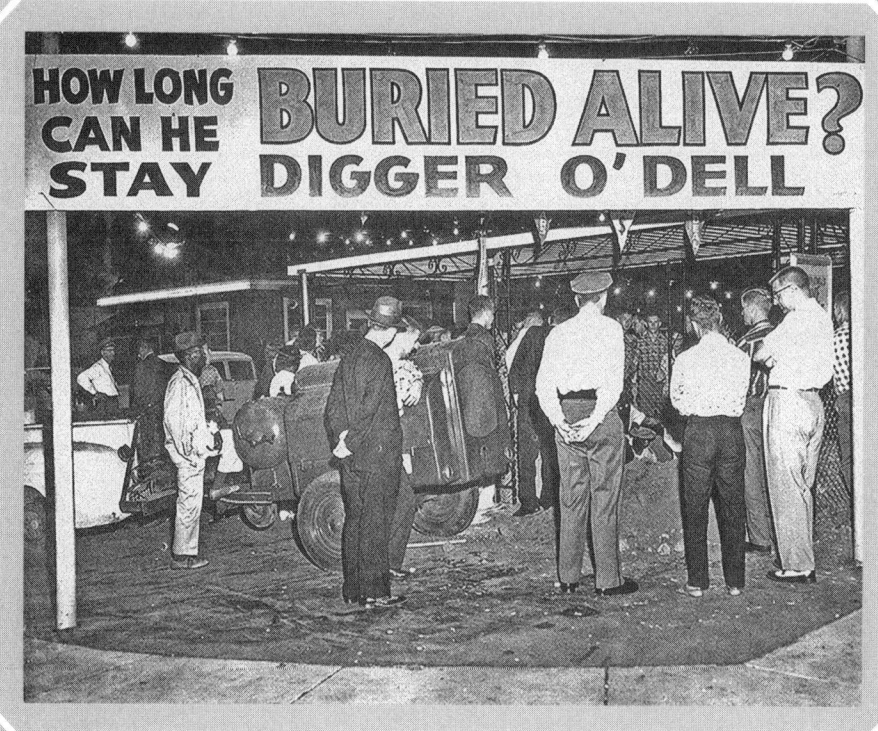

Digger O'Dell buried alive in Memphis, TN, ca. 1961. O'Dell traveled the south, including a visit to one of Cas Walker's grocery stores, performing his "buried alive" stunt. Memphis Public Library and Information Center.

CHAPTER 3

"Digger O'Dell—Buried Alive"

Perhaps the biggest promotion of Cas Walker's career involved burying a man in front of his Chapman Highway grocery store. Nearly every person I asked about "Digger O'Dell" had a story about seeing the stuntman six feet underground. However, no two stories are the same. Though reports vary, O'Dell spent almost three weeks in the ground sometime in the early 1960s before he "got to smotherin'," as Larry Mathis described it. While memories about the details of the stunt vary, some things are for sure: the promotion halted traffic, attracted hundreds of people, and made Cas thousands of dollars. Others indicate that the event was not worth the gasoline it took to drive over to South Knoxville to peer down at Digger.

"People Came from Everywhere"

★ *Knoxville News-Sentinel,* November 8, 1996

"In Days Before Cable, Local TV Supplied Long-Lasting Highlights" by Walker Johnson

I can remember a time in my life when there was no television. I don't mean a set; I mean stations. Young people often gather around my knee and ask, "Just what did you do before MTV?"

I tell them if they will get my shawl and pour me another shot of Metamucil, I can sum up life without TV in one word: Boring.

When our set did show up, we could get only one channel, and it was from Chattanooga. Over the years Knoxville came online with its stations. I grew up with "Cas Walker," "Mary Starr," "Bonny Lou and Buster," and "Clayton Star Time." These were locally produced shows, and the personalities that grew from these humble beginnings became Knoxville's media elite.

The granddaddy of the shows was "The Cas Walker Farm and Home Hour" on WBIR. . . . My favorite show was when he told everyone to come out and see a man buried alive at the Chapman Highway store. Cas hired a guy named Digger Odell, whose act was to be buried alive for a few days in your parking lot. Customers could come by and talk with Digger while he was underground. There was a shaft down to his head, and you could actually see Digger under the sod. For a few extra dollars he would allow snakes to be buried in the coffin with him. Cas hired Digger and the snakes, put him six feet under, and people came from everywhere to see him.

Years later, Cas spoke to a UT class I was attending and gave us the inside on Digger. He said that after a few days Digger wanted up, but sales at that one store were up 40 percent due to Digger and the snakes, so Cas didn't want to end the promotion. Here's the bottom line: When you are six feet under in a box with snakes, you come up when the man with the backhoe says you come up. Cas said he would talk to Digger late at night when the crowds were gone and offer him more money to stay interred, but all Digger wanted was out. When Cas finally dug him up, Digger took the cash and retired from show business.

★ Jack Sharp

I guess you've heard about Digger O'Dell.

This is when I was a teenager, driving, we were running around all over the city. I was dating my wife. . . . As you've been told, they dug a hole in the ground. And Digger O'Dell was down in there. And they had a glass box, that you could go in, and people would come over and look down in the box because that's where he was. I don't remember how many days he was down there.

A bunch of us—my wife was with me that night—and it was cold, it turned cold that night. And we went over there after we were not supposed to. As teenagers, we were gonna push it a little bit. And we got to peckin' on the glass panel on top. Trying to wake him up. We were pecking and hollering, "Digger, wake up, get up!"

Next thing I know, somebody had their hand on my shoulder and I turned around, and it was Cas!

He said, "Sharp, leave now." That's all he ever said. I got back in the car and drove off. He was tough. He could be scary. He had that old rough voice.

★ Bennie Wallen Jean

Digger O'Dell volunteered to do it; he did not have to. He was buried right across the street and they piped in air to him, I think. And people would go by and throw money in there, and, see, Mr. Walker's getting a lot of money there. Of course, he was paying that guy to stay under there and I forget how long he stayed under there, but the man got kinda claustrophobic and he was really wanting to get out before his contract ended, but Mr. Walker wouldn't let him. I think, after hours or something they got him out a little bit. A lot of people criticized Mr. Walker for that, but I didn't because the guy volunteered to do it.

It was really interesting, I went by about every day; I never did throw money. He was laying there fully clothed, and he was just laying there, you know, like he was dead. Just laying still.

I never did throw any money in because I thought, "He's getting paid anyway," but a lot of people would throw pennies in there and nickels. I wish I could remember how long he was under there.

★ Larry Mathis

My goodness, lot of people would come from all over. You can just imagine—"buried alive!" And they did, they put asphalt over the top, they sealed him in. He had a glass window that you could look down in there and it had lights down in there to work.

But ol' Digger got to smothering; he couldn't get enough air. So Cas went to Westinghouse or G.E. and got him an air conditioner. And he charged the company to say that Digger was being cooled by their air conditioner—Cas was always making money. Everything he done was for money.

But anyway, he still got to smothering, claustrophobia or something, and he wanted to be dug up. Cas said, "I ain't gonna dig him up, he's bringing too much business in!"

They had a nurse that would go over there and check his vitals and everything.

★ James Bragg

Was he buried with snakes?

I've heard the story from somebody. I was a kid. And I remember going up the steps to look down in it. They had a kind of platform where you could go. It was a glass box and you could look down and see the guy just laying down there. That's what I saw.

He was buried in a box. I'm sure they fed him and watered him. But I was thinking that there was something down there with him, but maybe I've seen too many TV shows.

★ Bo Pierce

They had a tube coming out for air; he could yell and I guess they could yell back at him. He had started getting claustrophobic and he was wanting out. I guess the rumors started going through the crowd and stuff.

Cas told me he got a bunch of his girls that worked checkout and whatever for his store, and bought some white nurses' outfits and put them in nurses' outfits and had them out there running around like it was really heightening up the tension, something's gonna happen, this guy's gonna die in Cas's parking lot!

★ David West

You oughta been there. They almost blocked the highway a few times. I think he had to have the law there for the traffic. People came [from] high and low. You know they're gonna buy something: "Let's go in there and get us a Coke." He had all kinds of promotions and things set up.

Mr. Walker said the guy stayed in there, he didn't stay the whole time, I forgot the exact amount of days, but after about ten days, $1,000, this guy's already rich and he was wanting out of there.

Mr. Walker's story: "I know what happened. He and his wife, they both were young and she was wanting him home for other reasons besides the money. They done had enough money to get out of town on, but I didn't wanna give him up because that store's doing so many thousands a day."

Digger said, "Well, I'm smothering down here."

Cas said, "Don't worry about it, I'll make you some ventilation."

He had them drill and put in a six-inch stove pipe down there close to him. Put a big wash tub down there, and he said, "I got looking at that, and I said, 'that's a waste of money.'"

He built a little roof over it and put in a wishing well. He said it took in over a hundred dollars a day in the wishing well, people dropping quarters down there! I guess they thought it was going to that guy, but it was going to Cas Walker.

He said, "You know I paid him off from the money in the wishing well!"

★ Bob Booker

I went to see Digger O'Dell one night. I had read all this hype and saw it on Cas's TV show. So I motored out on Chapman Highway just to see Digger O'Dell. And sure enough, there was this man down in the ground in this hole that had been dug. I think there might have been a glass top on it, and I think air was pumped in there and all of that.

It was hyped to the heavens but when you got there it was kind of disappointing. It's just a guy in a hole in the ground! It was no big deal. I wasted my gas going on Chapman Highway to see him.

★ Bruce Wheeler

Digger O'Dell—apparently, he went from town to town and he would sell this notion to usually a local grocer, and he would then be buried. And there was a pipe that ran down from—I don't know how deep the hole actually was—and he could either get air, but he said you could also pour soup down it. You could buy cans of soup—and he would heat them up and pour them down the thing. It was wild. . . .

When they brought him up, it was the same time that President Eisenhower was coming to the railroad station, and apparently there were more people in that parking lot to see Digger O'Dell be exhumed than were actually at the Southern Railway Station. That could well be true.

★ *Metro Pulse*, July 30, 1998, by Betty Bean (Excerpt)

All that's left of Digger Odell's Grave is a rough patch of asphalt in a parking lot on Chapman Highway. You have to look hard to find it. But for about a week in 1960, it was the most talked about spot in town—a literal traffic stopper.

It started when Digger talked Cas Walker into burying him alive. The result was spotlights and disc jockeys and big crowds peering at a man way down a hole while Walker dispensed popcorn and Cokes and barbecue.

There was a corrugated metal thing that mean little boys, compelled by the unshakable conviction that he had snakes down there with him, would scrape sticks across to drive Digger even crazier than he already was. . . .

The Digger Odell incident is just one of the many oddball P.R. exploits Cas Walker employed to promote his grocery stores, but it's also one of the most infamous. In his immodestly titled, self-published autobiography *My Life History, A True Living Legend,* Walker says it was Digger himself who presented the stunt as a unique promotional idea.

> "He said he wanted to be buried alive in front of one of the Cas Walker stores, preferably the one right there (on Chapman Highway).
> "I said 'How do you get a job like that?'
> He said 'I will be buried, six feet underground, with a stovepipe running down to where I am so people can talk to me.'
> I said, "What do you get for that kind of work?"
> He said "I get $100 a day."
> I said "I was thinking about offering you $25 a day, but I am going to offer you $50."
> His wife was a Jewish woman and she was shaking her head yes so I knew I was going to start burying a man and I had never had that experience before.
> We dug our hole, and I got ready to bury him. Of course, I advertised that I was going to bury him at a certain time. You never seen a crowd like we had."

Digger had a telephone, and Walker remembers that he "talked with women all night. You have never experienced a ladies man such as this one was." Walker put up a tent over Odell's grave to accommodate the crowd, which one night numbered 1,500 at 2 a.m.

But Digger wanted to be dug up before he had fulfilled his 30-day contract. Walker was having none of it, since daily receipts at the Chapman Highway store had increased from $3,500 to $8,000.

"I told him that was too much money to dig up," Walker said in a 1990 interview with the Knoxville Journal.

Digger started faking heart attacks and calling the newspapers and the health department to complain that Walker was denying him medical care.

Walker's solution was to dress two women who worked for him in "nurse suits" and station them above the grave, selling barbecued chicken sandwiches.

Again from Walker's autobiography: "Now this fellow [*Walker never mentions his name*], if there ever has been a trouble maker, he is number one. He got to smothering for no reason in the world, but I got my farm man to bring his post hole diggers and dig a hole at the foot of his grave. He got the hole dug and I got an 8 inch stove pipe and run down to the foot of his casket, and let it stick up out of the ground."

When people started throwing money down the pipe, wishing-well fashion, Walker in the digressing fashion that was his signature, says he "got the idea to work to raise money for needy children, so they could have milk. After two years working this fund, we furnished milk to every needy child in the city and the county, too. . . . I put a funnel in the stove pipe and a sign that said "Wishing Well" on it. They got real busy then. We took it up, we have $1,017. We gave it to the milk fund.

"This fellow in the grave called a doctor. He said he was smothering. Of course, he was under contract to the Cas Walker stores. The doctor took his temperature which showed to be 105. We drug along for 4 or 5 days, then we dug him up. He went to the Andrew Johnson Hotel and got a room. A nurse took his temperature when he got out of the grave and it was normal. About 15 or 20 women backed up trying to get into his room. This was the best promotion we ever had. The next best was Elvis Presley's will."

(Which is another story entirely . . .)

A Postscript to the Digger O'Dell Story

★ *Knoxville News-Sentinel*, March 25, 1980

"Digger Buried for U.S. Hostages"

Hubert O'Dell Smith, [a] stuntman who was buried alive at a Cas Walker supermarket here in August 1975 [*sic*], has been buried in Chattanooga, promising to remain underground until Iran releases the American hostages being held in the U.S. Embassy in Teheran.

Known as "Digger O'Dell" Smith, 64, from Cumming, Ga., he was buried in front of a Chattanooga car dealership which is sponsoring the effort. He says this is the 160th time he has been buried, either to make a living or to raise money for charity. He said his longest underground stay was 79 days. He was buried here for 21 days.

His six-foot deep grave houses a small television, chemical toilet and two telephones, one for calls from the general public and the other a private line for interviews with reporters. Food and water are to be lowered to Smith through a plywood chute which also permits ventilation. An intercom gives him 24-hour contact with an above-ground guard.

Cleaning the Western Avenue store after severe weather, August 8th, 1963. Printed by permission of the *Knoxville News Sentinel*.

CHAPTER 4

"I Work for Cas Walker"

Over the course of his life, Cas employed hundreds of people. While some Knoxvillians met the man on television and radio, perhaps the best insights into his character come from those who worked as cashiers, butchers, secretaries, and entertainers in Cas's media empire. This chapter gathers some of the recollections, fond and otherwise, of Walker's employees.

"The Biggest Compliment"

★ Rowdy Cope

He paid me the biggest compliment I've ever had. I was at the Lexington horse sale. We sold a lot of horses that day. I had $6,500 and I put it in a jacket pocket, and I was driving his '56 Chevrolet truck, and I had to come back to Knoxville. I came back to Knoxville without a stop. I didn't even stop for the bathroom because I didn't wanna take a chance on that money.

I went to his door over there on Gaston Avenue. Knocked on the door. Mr. Walker came to the door there, in his bathrobe.

I said, "Mr. Walker, I've got all this money. We sold those horses at Lexington. I don't want to keep it overnight."

He said OK.

I handed it to him wadded up in a roll.

Know what he done? He stuck it in his bathrobe pocket and said, "I'll see you tomorrow." He didn't even think about counting it or asking how much it was. He knew that I wouldn't steal a penny from him. That is a compliment from him, for that much money.

★ Bennie Wallen Jean

I was at UT, and I was doing my English paper on country music. So I went down to WIVK to interview him and I talked with him at length and took notes. I just went in there. Mr. Walker never made an appointment. The waiting room would be just full of people, and he'd just take 'em as they come: "Come on in!" He never had an appointment, never made appointments.

Anyway, I talked to him, and then he said, "Would you like to have a job?" I was kinda stunned. He said, "I really need a good bookkeeper."

I said, "Well, I'm still in school, but I'll think about it."

He said, "Well, when you get ready to go to work, come see me."

I thanked him and I left. Then I came to Knoxville in the fall to register for second year of UT and so as I was walkin' down Gay Street, I saw the National Business College and it said, "Earn a degree in bookkeeping secretarial work in nineteen months." And the nineteen months was re-registering in my head so I went a couple blocks, and then I turned around and I came back.

I thought, "Well, I'm gonna investigate this." I went upstairs and talked to them and they convinced me that that's what I should do. I go home and I tell my parents. They hit the ceiling! My daddy said, "If you do that don't ever ask me for another penny." I said, "I won't."

They wanted me to go ahead and finish school. They didn't want that. But that turned out to be the best thing ever was.

So anyway, when I got a little certificate I trekked off then to the radio station and showed Mr. Walker my certificate, and he said, "I want you to work for my bookkeeper at Tennessee Valley Advertising Agency. I need a bookkeeper there and a secretary. You'll be my secretary."

He said, "Before you start, I'm gonna send you to the North Central Store. I'm gonna call Kevin, he's the manager, and I want you to learn every aspect of the grocery business."

You talk about fright! I thought, "I don't know if I wanna do the job or not."

But I go—and I couldn't figure in my mind: "Why do I need to do this?" But I went out there and Kevin was very nice, and first day they taught me how to bag groceries, and to this day, I just get ruffly feathers when I go in the store and they're doin' it wrong! Sometimes I even say, "Hey, you don't do that!" So there is an art to bagging groceries.

The next day I helped 'em take inventory. Then I learned how to cut meat. Then I learned the head cashier's business. In a week's time, I knew the grocery business, and it was invaluable training. I mean, all the stuff I learned in the grocery store!

I really liked that job, it was the best job I ever had. I enjoyed it to the fullest because it was different every day, never boring. Always had a lot of work to do, more than I could do, but I did it!

When I left, Mr. Walker got up on the TV and he said, "I didn't know my secretary worked so hard." He'd call my name and he said, "I had to hire two people to replace her!" But it didn't dawn on him to hire a person when I was keepin' it up!

★ Ben Walker

I'll tell ya this one more story about me, too. I worked for him at Broadway, and it was a rainy day. Usually I was stock boy and bag boy; I didn't run the cash register. He had four cash registers up front and two in the rear of the store. One of the girls didn't show up so they told me to sit on the back register 'til they showed up.

It was rainin' hard and not very many people were in the store, so I did the cigarettes and the candy bars, straighten up everything, and done what I could, and then there was nothin' else to do so I just got me a newspaper and spread it out on the counter.

And I was just readin' and he come in the back door and he just didn't say a word. Went to the office, got on the intercom, and said, "If certain employees cannot read the paper before they leave home for the morning, I would just as soon that they stay home."

I got so mad. And he went out the front door—he didn't go out the back, 'cause I woulda jumped on him!

★ Cas Walker, *My Life History*

The Employee Who Slugged His Way to the Top

One time an employee came in late and I asked him where he had been. He said he had been to a chiropractor. I said, "A chiropractor, the devil, there are customers in here and you've been there!" Whew! I had seen things that should have been done and that weren't, I guess I got mad.

I now know that it was a mistake on my part, but I just kept asking him why he went. He said that he had permission to go. One word just started another, and it wound up that we got in an old fashion fist fight.

He was much of a man, but it hadn't been too long since I was working in the coal mines and I was as stout as a bull. I hit him a good solid blow and knocked him through one of the front windows of the store! He came a running back in and asked me who was going to pay for the window! I told him that I was going to pay for the window and for him to get on back there and wait on our customers and to come in the next morning to report as store manager. He turned out to be a good one.

This fellow has turned out to be a preacher, and if he fights as hard spiritually as he could physically, I'm sure he will be a champion for Jesus.

★ Becky Orange Dwarshuis

I was called to the office to take a gentleman down to meet Cas, and as I walked down the hall, the gentleman told me, "When I was a young man I served time in prison, and when I got out of prison, I was destitute, I did not have a penny. I had no job skills. But I heard that Cas Walker may give me a job. So I went in to the store. I said, 'Cas, I just got out of prison, I've paid my penalty. I will never commit another crime. If you'll have trust in me and give me a job, I promise you I'll be honest and I will be a good worker for you.'"

He told me that story as we were walkin' down the hall, and he said, "Before he dies and before I die, I just wanna look Cas Walker in the face and say, 'Thank you for giving me a chance.'"

So I knocked on the door, and Cas came. The man said, "He will never remember my name, he will never remember." There was a rumor floating around that he had Alzheimer's disease—he did *not* have Alzheimer's disease. We knocked on the door, and when Cas opened it, he said his name, and then he said, "You were the only man in Knoxville who could fix a broken buggy."

Here's what Cas told him. He said, "I'll give you a job. Go behind the store, I have these grocery buggies, and the wheels don't work. If you'll fix the wheels I'll pay you." I think he said it was a dollar a buggy. It might not have been. This gentleman said, "I had no job skills and I had never even pushed a buggy through a store. I had no idea what I was gonna do. So here I go. I push this—a broken buggy to my house"—he'd moved in with his mother—he said, "I had to borrow a screwdriver and a wrench," he said, "but that wasn't good enough, I had to walk back to the store and get another one so I could take the wheels off the one that worked." And he said, "That began a vocation for me," he said, "after I learned how to do that, I invested in some tools, I invested in some wheels." And he said, "When I made thirty dollars, when I saved up thirty dollars, I bought a truck."

And he said, "I never had to walk again."

And he said he went to the A&P and told them, "If you got any broken buggies I'll fix your buggies." And he went to the White store, and he said, "I had all the buggies I could fix and I had plenty of money." He said, "That's all I ever did and it was all because Cas trusted in me enough." He said, "I was an ex-con with no vehicle, and Cas gave me the opportunity to have a good life."

And he said, "When I would meet people they would say, 'What do you do now?'" And he said, "I would answer *with pride*, 'I work for Cas Walker.'"

Job Interview

★ Jane Bandy Shuler

In the summer of 1968, I had just graduated from UT with a degree in journalism and was looking for a job. When I saw an ad posted in the *News-Sentinel* by Tennessee Valley Advertising Agency looking for someone with "good communication skills," I called to ask for a job interview. I was surprised to learn when I called that Tennessee Valley Advertising Agency was owned by Cas Walker, who answered the phone himself. After four years of living in Knoxville while attending UT, I was familiar with Cas Walker's brand of journalism and thought I wanted no part of it, but I *did* need a job, so I went to the interview.

Tennessee Valley Advertising Agency was located in a small brick building just off Chapman Highway near the Cas Walker Grocery Store. After a few minutes of talking with Cas Walker, it became apparent that what he wanted was not someone to write press releases and advertising copy, but someone to answer his office telephone, and the low salary he was planning to pay would barely cover my rent. As I continued to answer his questions with very little focus on what he was asking because I was trying to figure out how to gracefully end this interview for a job I did not intend to accept even if it was offered to me, he surprised me with, "Are you a good girl?"

That certainly got my attention, and was such an unexpected question that my response was "What?"

"Do you sleep around?" he replied.

At this point I suddenly realized that I was a young girl alone with a much older man in a somewhat isolated location. Was he concerned about the moral standards of his potential employees—or had he just propositioned me? In a situation that had suddenly become decidedly creepy, I quickly assured him that I was not sexually promiscuous and got out of there as fast as I could politely exit.

Years later, that long-ago job interview comes back to me—Cas Walker, the only potential employer who ever asked me about my sex life.

A Firing Legend

★ Bradley Reeves

I've heard so many stories about Cas Walker, so many, and a lot of them come from different places but they're the same story, and you wonder, hmm, that's kind of been absorbed into legend, and people embellish it, add to it, subtract it. The time Cas came into his grocery store and there was a fellow leaning up against the counter, talking to one of his beautiful workers, flirting. He says, "Give that boy his last paycheck, tell him to get out of here."

And the guy gets his money and he leaves, and the lady said, "Well, he didn't work here."

I've heard that story so many times. I don't know how true that is.

★ Carter G. Baker

Major Temple Scalf (known as Temple) worked as a butcher at one of Cas Walker's Knoxville grocery stores. In fact he stayed with Cas till the stores closed back in the 1980s. Temple had several Cas Walker stories, but I only remember one of them.

Temple started with Cas right out of high school as a sack boy. Sack boys wore a white butcher's apron and were warned that if Cas ever saw them sitting down, they would be summarily fired. He wanted everyone who worked for him busy all the time—bagging groceries, sweeping the lot, or spiffing up the shelves.

Temple had a friend who worked at a drugstore across the street, and they would often meet to eat a sandwich together. The drugstore boys wore a similar apron so one day as his friend sat on the front window sill waiting for Temple to go on his break, Cas walked in. When he spied a young man in a white apron sitting down in express disregard of his orders, he lost his temper.

"I've told you bastards I don't want you sitting down in my stores. You're fired right now!" And with that he reached in his pocket, pulled out a ten-dollar bill, and thrust it at the boy telling him to get the hell out. Without allowing Temple's friend to explain, he stalked off looking for another miscreant.

Friend took his new-found wealth, scampered out the door, and became a bit player in yet another Cas Walker legend—firing someone who didn't even work for him!

★ James Bragg

Here's a good story. You ever hear about him firing a White store guy? Cas told me this story himself, whether he embellished it or whatever. But he says, "I ever tell you about the time I fired a White store worker?"

"No."

Well, he went into his store down on Magnolia. And there was a White store down the street. There was a young man sitting up there on the counter drinking a Coke. Had a white apron on.

He went up to him and said, "How much do you make an hour?"

He said, "I make $1.80," or whatever it was.

And he said, "How many hours did you work this week?"

He says, "Twenty-five."

Cas goes to his office girl and has her come out and says, "Give this guy a check, he's fired."

He says, "But Mr. Walker!"

He says, "You're loitering, you need to be working."

So he fired a guy that had come down there to visit one of his buddies that was at the store.

Cas at Wile-o-Diner, December 11, 1943. Printed by permission of the *Knoxville News Sentinel*.

CHAPTER 5

"The Guy Literally Was Everywhere"

A Pioneer of Radio and TV

By the 1950s, Cas Walker was one of the region's most visible media personalities, first on radio and then on television sets throughout East Tennessee. It was here that Cas crossed paths with Dolly Parton, the Acuff and Carter families, and the Everly Brothers. Indeed, some argue that Cas Walker's program was the first showcase and springboard for many talented performers who went on to perform in Nashville and the Grand Ole Opry. This chapter shows how Cas Walker used the explosion in American media at mid-century to promote his country-boy persona to a broader region, which made Walker one of Appalachia's unavoidable icons.

The "Farm and Home Hour"

★ *Metro Pulse*, September 30, 1998, by Betty Bean (Excerpt)

For anyone past the age of 25, no memory of an East Tennessee childhood is complete without a *Cas Walker's Farm and Home Hour* vision of Red Rector's Vienna-sausage fingers flying over the mandolin strings and Honey Wilds' big mitts whaling on the little ukulele he called his chili dipper. There were David West's hot banjo licks and clear as yesterday morning, Curly Dan Bailey's high, lonesome tenor soaring on the "Do your grocery shopping" part of the *Farm and Home Hour* theme song, with yodeling Claude Boone calling out, "Say that again," and all of them standing in front of the big painting of Cas treeing a whole family of coons and joining in to harmonize on the "... at a Cas Walker store" finale.

David West, now the owner of Ciderville Music Barn, laughs when he remembers some of the God-awful cloggers and gospel singers Walker would let on the show: "Fred Smith always said The Gong Show got their idea from Cas Walker. He'd put people on that couldn't sing a lick." (In his defense, Walker did give Dolly Parton her first break . . . and also famously kicked the Everly Brothers off his show.)

There's Cas in a porkpie hat waving his hands and pointing at his merchandise with his crooked middle finger—a habit and a deformity that launched a million adolescent locker room jokes. And everybody knows somebody who can imitate that gravelly voice flogging merchandise: "Neighbors, we've got these number one–grade Mrs. Paul's fish filets . . ." or Bush's pinto beans or Blue Band Coffee (which was really JFG packaged up as Cas' house brand).

Walker was on Channel 10 for 30 years, selling stuff and threatening dog thieves and blasting his political enemies and taking up money for the Milk Fund or for some family in Dumplin Valley that got burnt out over the weekend.

The Farm and Home Hour was on the air until March 30, 1983, when Channel 10 pulled the plug.

"I remember I cried," Boone says.

★ Jeff Ross

When my father mustered out of the army in 1973, he came to Knoxville to close on a house in Holston Hills. My mother and I (who was four at the time) left Germany, where my father was stationed, and came to Knoxville a few weeks later. My father had to report back to Texas to finish the discharge, which left my mother and me alone in a strange city. Our new house wasn't yet ready to move into, so we stayed for a time in the Scottish Inn hotel on Asheville Highway. The day after we arrived was a Saturday, so my mother, who knew nothing of the South and didn't exactly want to be away from her home in Colorado, turned on the TV as a distraction. The first thing she saw was the Cas Walker *Farm and Home Hour*. This was to be her initiation to East Tennessee. She broke down sobbing, sure that if he was a television star, then the rest of Knoxville was the same or worse.

She longed to be gone from here, but eventually grew to love Knoxville, and lived here for the next forty years.

Cas with Mules on the "Farm and Home Hour" set at WBIR in Knoxville, ca. 1960s.

★ Bradley Reeves

WNOX was right down the street here, and so much great talent came out of here, almost all of them ended up in Nashville. Because folks here didn't promote it enough. A lot of the city fathers, or the silk stocking crowd, were kind of embarrassed of it. Our radio stations didn't have the wattage of Nashville. WSM could be heard all over the country on a nice night.

WNOX tried. They had a show here called the "Midday Merry-Go-Round." Chet Atkins, Roy Acuff, Don Gibson, the Carter Sisters, Mother Maybelle. The list is astounding, and almost all of them went away by the '50s because that's where the music scene was happening. If you wanted to make a living you had to go to Nashville.

It kind of died for a while during the '60s during the rock and roll era when Elvis came along and everything changed. But so much great talent came out of here.

Cas, he fed into that. He gave these people a chance. That's how he fed the machine, constantly. If you look at the newspaper clippings of the time: "Cas will be on at 6:30 on WIVK; Cas will be on at noon at WROL." He was there and people would keep that station on WROL and listen to him throughout the day, or they would switch to wherever he was.

His role in hiring musicians—I'll give you an example. So many collections have come into TAMIS [the Tennessee Archive of Moving Image and Sound]—photographs, memorabilia, things that people have kept over the years. Cas is almost in every one of them. Somewhere, there's either a picture of him or an autograph, or "tune into the Cas Walker Show to hear so-and-so."

He was that prevalent, and people really did look to him for music, musical taste, their politics, political views. He was a very important man.

★ David West

We had the number one show! . . . He went to bed at 11 o'clock, he got up at 3:00. He'd tell me, "Don't call me after 11, don't call me before 3:00."

He got up at 3:00 o'clock and had his coffee, I guess, and he turned on the news stations, and he read the newspaper. "Pick up the morning paper." It came out early, he was on the *Journal*, the early morning paper. He read it, he was a speed-reader.

He read the newspaper, he was done up before everybody else, and when he went on TV, he could broadcast what was in the paper before anybody else got the paper!

A lot of people didn't buy the paper, they'd say, "I'll just turn on the Cas Walker Show! He knows everything that's good and everything that's bad."

★ Ben Walker

Everybody watched his show. I remember when it first came on, I can remember he had them playin' that bluegrass: "Pick up the mornin' paper when it hits the street, Cas Walker prices, they just can't be beat, try that Blue Band coffee and you'll want some more, do your grocery shoppin' at a Cas Walker store." That came on first thing!

★ Larry Mathis

At one time, in the '60s, he had probably the best entertainers in the whole country, around here, on there. And they were really good, they had good music, and he got to where he'd let *anything* come on there. It kind of left a dark cloud—because he had people like the Brewster Brothers and the Webster Brothers, they were as good as they come. They had little Robert, he was a fellow that was 39 inches tall. He was a normal man from his waist up and his legs were 11 inches long, that's all that they ever grew.

They had Robert Newton, a really good singer, and they had James Carson, they had Harold Harper, he was a great guitar player, wound up playing with Don Gibson at the Opry. They had Danny Bailey, and myself.

And later on Red Rector and Fred Smith came, and Honey Wilds came later on.

But what we'd do, we had a bass fiddle there, and if the Brewster Brothers played, one of us would just get up and play the bass behind them. We always helped back up each other. I sang a lot with the Webster Brothers and then Dan Bailey and I sang together, and the Brewster Brothers would sing together, and then the Brewster Brothers and the Webster Brothers had what they called the Four Brothers Quartet. Later on, it was the Cas Walker Quartet.

And then Cas would get somebody on there that couldn't carry a tune in a tow sack. And Cas would just put them on because them people had people. Trade—it was all in the back of Cas's mind.

★ James Bragg

When I was in first grade, we had a talent contest. Our gym doubled as our auditorium. I remember seeing Cas Walker, 'cause his grandsons went to that school too.

I was with three other guys. We dressed up like little train engineers and we sang "I've Been Working on the Railroad." Well, we didn't win the competition. Another group, some baton twirlers, won it.

He invited the baton twirlers to be on his show, and I guess because I'm his nephew he invited us on it too. So, we got to sing "I've Been Working on the Railroad" on the Cas Walker show. So that's my claim to fame. That was fun.

★ David West

Now, anybody that came in there, you did no audition—he'd put you on. He'd put everybody on because his theory was everybody buys groceries. You've got a kid, or she's got a kid, and you took your daughter or your son in there, and he treated them nice and put them on TV, well, you're gonna talk about Cas Walker!

He said he made more money by making friends sometimes than he could by advertisement.

★ Bradley Reeves

Great ear for music, but he let anybody on the show, that was his downfall sometimes. He'd let his neighbor's cousin on without any kind of an audition. There are some clips that are just unspeakable. You could only watch them late at night, with the curtains drawn and the doors locked, because they're so bad. . . .

Later on, in the '60s, a lot of the hippies, they'd smoke marijuana and watch him and laugh at the TV screen. . . . It's out of this world!

Dolly Parton and Cas

★ Ben Walker

Now I will tell you this: when I was seventeen or eighteen, I've got two nieces the same age I am, and they sang, so Cas used to have a studio down on South Gay Street. I think it was WIVK. And every day at eleven o'clock, he had a show down there. And my nieces used to go down there, and he would let them sing every once in a while, on his show. But one time we went down there, and this little girl was there and she was eleven years old, and she sang. And when we left, we were goin' back up the street, and I said, "That girl had a funny voice," and it was Dolly Parton! She was just about eleven years old.

★ Becky Orange Dwarshuis

My parents would see Dolly on there and say, "Oh, that poor child! Put her back in the bed and let her rest!" The roads from Sevier County to Knoxville were curvy and they had to get up real early before she went to school. And she did look exhausted, but I will say she never messed up. If she ever messed up, they would put that on TV all the time. She learned her lines and she stayed on key. And sometimes she looked like she was a little ragged child. But she never missed her words. You can ask David West about that. In addition to perfecting her skill, it was a natural ability with her. Because one time on the show, someone was singing "Little Brown Jug," and he forgot the words. And he said—it was an older man—he said, "I learned this song when I was a little boy by my daddy; I've never forgotten it. And I forgot it!" And he said, "I apologize." Dolly never forgot her lines. Never.

★ Rowdy Cope

He kinda took a shine to Dolly. I was up at the television station the first morning she showed up. Dolly Parton.

We was giving a pony away at one of the stores, and I took the pony in before Dolly went in. It was in November 1956. Dolly went in to sing, and the pony pooped all over in there. It didn't faze her, she just stepped over the poop and went to the microphone and sang.

She had a little pink dress on—she was nine years old, I was thirteen. I put my jacket around her shoulders to keep her from freezing to death because we had to stay outside until it came time to go on.

He just took a shine to her. And she climbed greasy poles and all kinds of stuff and went and done a lot of shows with him.

He put her with Porter Wagner. Actually, Mr. Walker told Loretta Lynn, "If you didn't carry them kids around with you all the time, you might make it."

★ Becky Orange Dwarshuis

When Dolly would meet Cas, on a personal level, after she became famous and after he became elderly, she would run and sit in his lap, and she would say, "Cas, it ain't a fur piece from Knoxville to Nashville, is it?" And he would say, "Dolly, for you it was not."

Here's what happened. He had a driver—sometimes it was David West— and he said, "We had to go to Nashville, but we were gonna be like five men in the car and we all smoked cigars. Dolly hated cigars and it would make her carsick and give her a headache and everything."

So he said, "I promised her the next time I went I would take her. But I was goin' with all these men and cigars and I knew she probably wouldn't wanna go." But she heard that they were goin' so she said, "Cas, you're goin' to Nashville, ain't ya? I wanna go with ya." And he said, "The car'll be full of cigars, Dolly, you don't need to go with us."

"Yes, I do. Never been to Nashville, I wanna go."

So they got in the car; they left real early. Dolly never slept a minute late in her life, and I'm not sure how old she was; she was not a little child at this point. He said, "We put her up front so she wouldn't get carsick"—the driver, Dolly, and Cas.

"We were not out of Knoxville until," he said, "I could feel her little body relaxing and she fell sound asleep." And he said, "I motioned to the men in the backseat: 'she's sleeping.'" And he said, "All the way to Nashville I sat up and I just let her sleep on me, and right before we had to get out of the car in Nashville I woke her up, and she said, 'Oh, Cas, it ain't a fur piece from Knoxville is it?'"

And he said, "Dolly, for you it was not a fur piece."

The Greasy Pole

★ Cas Walker, *My Life History*

Dolly and the Greasy Pole

Dolly was always a good person, down to earth and with the knack of wanting to be a success. She runs Dollywood now, and I always go over on opening day, and we still communicate by writing letters.

She married a pretty good boy and he goes with her if it's around close, but he just don't care for going off away from home.

When Dolly was little and television came in, she went over great. She goes over great today.

I had rented a place up in Sevierville and we started a show. Business had been slow up there. I paid fifty dollars a month rent on this old theatre building. I used some ideas and events that I used for store openings. I had a greasy pole climbing contest.

I took a pole about fifty feet long. I dug a hole in the floor and put the pole in it with concrete around the bottom. We greased it down and I put fifty dollars on top. Every Saturday night, my God, the place would be packed! The pole kept bringing people back, they knew they would get to the top next time.

Dolly was about six or seven years old and she tried to climb it every weekend. She wore a pair of little overhalls [*sic*], and she could sing and bring the house down! She had been doing some studying about that pole, and she was actually smarter than me, because she figured out a way to climb the pole and get my money. I couldn't figure out how to climb it, but she did.

She had her mother take her down to the river, and she waded out and got wet. She came back to the shore and rolled in a sandbar and had grit and sand all over her clothes. I kept watching for her and she came and was by the door. She looked all ruffed [*sic*] up and I wondered what happened to her. She came up to the pole and went straight up to the top like a squirrel! She got the fifty dollars and broke up my greasy pole contest.

Everyone knew then how Dolly climbed that pole and of course we couldn't use it anymore.

I later had a trick horse whom we named Dolly, and you know who we named it after.

★ Larry Mathis

I'm sure you've heard of the greasy pole. Have you ever heard of that? All right, let me tell you this. See, Cas told that he put up a greasy pole and Dolly climbed it and got the money.

Now, here's what happened. Willy Brewster and Fred Smith decided that they were gonna put a jamboree on up at the Pines Theater in Sevierville.

They came up with the idea of a greasy pole. Now, in the summertime, you can go up and cut like a poplar tree and when the sap is up, you can take that tree and when it lays down you can cut a little groove through the bark. They've got what they call a spud. It's just a little ol' thing, made kind of like a kitchen spatula, but it was made with a three-foot handle and out of metal. And you could get it under that bark and when the sap was up it would peel all that bark off. Of course, the pole was slick at that time and poplars didn't have many limbs on them, they might could cut one that was twenty-five feet high without a limb.

So, they came up with the idea. Willie G.'s older brother cut the pole, and he brought it up to Sevierville and put it up. Probably nailed it to the floor. That's the greasy pole, the poplar tree. It's about seven or eight inches through. Bigger than a two-liter Coke bottle, but not too awful big.

Anyhow, what they would do—of course there wasn't money on top of it—but it was if you can climb it to the top, you get, they had like $500. Well, what they would do, they'd start out and they could climb maybe the first two or three feet. Willie and them would put Crisco shortening and the higher up they got, the more shortening. You'd climb up a foot and slide back two, the higher you got.

And there was nobody, nobody, nobody, *ever* climbed that greasy pole. But the people would come out, and they would try to with all their might. They also went to the stores, furniture stores and got lamps and maybe a small TV or something, bicycles, they had all kinds of prizes. It just drew everybody in. But nobody ever climbed it.

But Cas, I don't know how in the world that he came up with this, and I know that this did *not* happen. You will hear stories about this, that Dolly was little and she went down and got in the creek and got her clothes wet and then rolled in the sand and came up and climbed. *That never happened.* I don't care who tells you it did, it never—you ask Bud Brewster, he was there from '54 or '55, he was there, and he'll tell you. And if Willie was alive he would tell you. And if Fred Smith—the last time we talked to Fred Smith, Bud and I went to see him before he died, and we were talking about that.

Fred said, "I don't care what they say. No, sir. Nobody ever climbed the greasy pole."

I don't know how Cas got this in his head or whether it was a sort of a little joke or something to get people to talk about it, I don't know. I don't think he would deliberately stand on both feet and lie about it unless it was just a fun thing, I don't know. But sometimes you hear stories like that.

"You Couldn't Escape Him"

★ Bradley Reeves

He rode with the times, going from the radio into television—he was right there. Talk about a pioneer in television! Nineteen fifty-three, the first year that television came to Knoxville, he was right there, he made this transition over to the visual medium, and what strikes me as interesting is at one time, this guy had television shows on WTSK-TV, I think that was a morning, early morning show, and then there was WBIR, which was an afternoon show, and then channel 6, WATE, which was an evening show, thirty-minute blocks.

So you hear stories of, "Well, he bought time on all three stations. You would just change the channel, you couldn't escape him, all three channels had Cas at the same time!"

No—it's a great story—but he was on different channels at different times during the day.

He also had radio at that time period, so he was doing radio on WKXV and radio on WROL. The guy literally was everywhere for decades. He was on the radio, he was on television, billboards—he was a media kingpin, and I don't know how he did it. I've heard that he used certain stimulants to keep going, back when they were legal. I think later on you had to get prescriptions for amphetamines, diet pills, what have you.

★ Bruce Wheeler

Red and Fred were on the Cas Walker show. When I first moved to Knoxville, there was a television ad that I think Red and Fred might have been the characters in. But it was the most outrageous ad, and they were sitting there and between them was a pig.

One of them said, "Who's that jackass you're talking to?"

The other one said, "That's not a jackass, that's a pig."

The other one said, "I was talking to the pig."

Then they said, "Cas Walker, potatoes, so and so" and on they would go.

Cas had this big easel on his set, and all of these prices and he would just throw them and then "here's another one" and then throw it. . . . They would have some music in the background and they would say, "It's the 'Cas Walker Farm and Home Hour.'" At the end, he was sitting down, and he had his tie that never quite got to his belt and he would say here's some of the things that are going on with me. Then he would introduce Red or Fred or the guests and they would go back to him. He would do a commercial. There wasn't much in the way of politics on the show.

Sometimes toward the end, Walker would meander into areas that were not groceries but weren't exactly politics either. Like the guy that had his car stolen, or somebody that needed a handout and that kind of thing.

★ Jerry Wing

The allegation was Cas would arrive at the studio quite properly dressed but just before the taping was to begin, he'd pull his tie askew, unbutton his suit coat and pull it askew so as to conform to his "country" image. Once the taping finished, he'd straighten his clothes and be on his way.

★ James Bragg

He had these 3×5 cards in his pocket, and he'd pull these things out and say, "Here at Cas Walker's we've got Del Monte Pizzas, three for a dollar."

Or he'd pull one out and go, "Well, I've got a guy up here in Poundville, Kentucky, he's got a dog," and he starts looking at it and playing with his glasses, and he starts reading the attributes of this coon dog, and he gets down to the name and he goes, "Whoa, wait a minute, that's my dog!"

He'd sell groceries, coon dogs, advice. It was funny.

Have you heard the roach killer story? This is my favorite Cas Walker story. He had a glass gallon jug of Blue Band Roach Killer, whatever brand it was. That was his store brand. In this gallon jug.

And I saw this on TV, I witnessed it. He's holding this jug, it's like 6:30 in the morning, I'm getting ready to go to school. He always had so many blunders that I had to watch it because it was fun, and we could laugh and talk about it. Maybe a lot of it was on purpose.

But he had this big jug, and he's telling them about all of the attributes of this jug of this roach killer. And he's pointing with his finger and it slipped out of his hands.

And the camera goes from his face while he was talking, and it goes right down, right at his feet is a broken glass, a gallon jug of roach killer, and he's got wet up here. And that camera goes right back up. And Cas, he didn't smile or anything, and then you think, "Did he do this on purpose?"

And he never lost his composure. But you can see Cas, he gets right back on the camera, and he says, "I'll tell you one thing, friends and neighbors, there'll be many a day before a roach crosses this stage and lives."

True story.

★ Larry Mathis

Back in the '40s and the '50s, farm people, they listened every morning or every day at lunch. The reason they had shows at 11:30 until 12:30 or 1:00, farmers were home eating lunch. Now, we called it dinner back then—it was breakfast, dinner, and supper. I don't know where they came in with this dinner at night. It's still supper to us.

But anyhow, the people loved that kind of music and of course, some people say that Cas was pretty colorful. I guess he was. I didn't agree with a lot of his politics and a lot of his doings and things like that, but he was very popular. If he ran for something, it's kind of like nowadays, he'd get elected, but you couldn't find nobody that voted for him.

What Cas said back then, these old-timers would chisel it in stone. They thought that that was the Gospel. If Cas said it, then it's gotta be right. He always liked that kind of music. That sold his groceries. When rock 'n' roll came out, he didn't like it. He said, "Kids don't buy groceries, Mom and Daddy buy groceries."

★ Betty Bean

I thought his TV show was just corny and embarrassing.

In the summertime, when my cousins would come from other parts of the country to visit, inevitably somebody would turn on TV in the morning, and there were times when Cas was on all three channels at once, competing with himself! So here would come the "Farm and Home Hour," in the morning with that high, lonesome music that I just considered whiny and nasal and irritating and country and embarrassing.

And he had cloggers, it seems like he had *a lot* of cloggers. They were little girls with big flouncy skirts and lots of crinoline and taps on their shoes and they'd do these weird kicks. A lot of times they'd show their underwear and show their panties, and it was just—oh God, it was embarrassing.

And Cas didn't cut them a lot of slack: if he didn't like them, he'd shuffle out there in the middle of their act and say, "That's enough of that!"

I considered myself too sophisticated for Cas. I was into rock 'n' roll, and I was into Fats Domino and Ricky Nelson.

★ *Knoxville News-Sentinel,* March 26–27, 1986 (Edited)

"The Last Patriarch of Local Country Music Was Cas Walker"
by Wayne Bledsoe

The 1950s and '60s marked the biggest successes and the biggest failures for East Tennessee's country music.

On one hand, performers like Don Gibson, The Everly Brothers, Carl Smith and Dolly Parton all became superstars. However, by the late '60s, local country music had nearly vanished. In Knoxville, the dominant force in country music moved from Lowell Blanchard to another local personality.

"Lowell was doing it to sell tickets, but I was doing it to sell groceries," says Cas Walker.

Walker started his "Farm and Home Hour" even before Blanchard started "The Midday Merry-Go-Round." It didn't take long before he was a firm believer in country music's power.

"Before we went on the air in 1929, I had never done $100,000 worth of business in a week. After we'd been on the air for one week, I did," Walker says. . . .

Known as "the millionaire grocer," Walker had always been a sharp businessman. When television came along, he hopped on board. His show went on the air in 1956 on WBIR-TV. Like his radio program it was called the "Farm and Home Hour," although it would run anywhere from 30 to 90 minutes. The show served a breakfast of country music, advertisements and political asides to anyone watching television early in the morning.

Walker covered all the bases. At one point during the '60s he had the show broadcast simultaneously on all three of Knoxville's television stations. "I'd tell them: 'Just change the channel if you don't like what's on here!'" said Walker. . . .

The first of his superstars was a young man from Maynardville named Carl Smith. Smith was still attending high school when he joined the show in the '40s, but he opened the '50s with a bang. His song "Let's Live a Little" shot up the country charts and even rescued an earlier song called "I Overlooked an Orchid" from slipping off the charts. In the next 15 years he had over 90 songs on the country charts. Sixty went into the top 10 and Smith says, "I really don't know how many went to No. 1."

Walker fired his next superstars in 1956 when they, in his words, "started playing that old rock 'n' roll stuff!" The husband and wife team Ike and Margaret Everly had performed on Walker's show for some time. Ike Everly was a respected guitarist from Kentucky, but it was the couple's sons, Don and Phil, that gave Walker a problem.

"Cas was always on them to cut their hair," remembers past Walker performer Pearl Butler.

"They were good boys," Walker says, "but I just had to let them go. I told them 'that wiggle wouldn't sell groceries.'"

The wiggle may not have sold groceries, but one year later when the Everlys moved to Nashville, they proved that it could sell records. Songs like

"Bye, Bye Love," "All I Have To Do Is Dream," "Wake Up Little Susie" and "Cathy's Clown" became monster hits and have since become classics. Thirty years later their music continues to influence country and rock music.

Carl and Pearl Butler left Walker's show for Nashville the same year that the Everlys became superstars, but Pearl was not always part of the act. "I went up and sang when I was on my lunch hour," says Pearl Butler. "I worked in the meat department at one of Cas' stores." When Carl Butler and his group, "The Lonesome Pine Boys," were asked to join the Grand Ole Opry in 1958, Pearl was still only performing occasionally. In 1962 they decided to record a song together. "Don't Let Me Cross Over (Love's Cheating Line)" stayed No. 1 for 27 weeks and their success continued well into the '70s. . . .

One of Walker's most popular performers was superstar Dolly Parton. Parton began her career with Walker at the age of 10 and stayed with the show until she graduated from high school. She was writing songs at the age of 5. By the age of 8 she was performing at the Pines Theater in Sevierville in one of Cas Walker's shows. When she was 10, Walker asked her to appear as a regular on his radio and television programs in Knoxville. She was also expected to perform at live shows in surrounding areas.

"Cas was wonderful," Parton says. "He always took care of me. You know he treated me like a child, but he talked to me like an adult."

Part of that talk was sound stage advice.

"He told me to look at that television camera like you're talking to an old friend," she recalls.

"People were always good to me and helped me along," says Parton. . . .

Now she is one of the highest paid performers in America. Her songs are instant hits, and she reportedly earns $350,000 a week when she performs in Las Vegas. . . .

When Parton left for Nashville in 1964, country music was at its nadir in Knoxville. Live radio had dried up. With fewer outlets for country performers, it became harder for local acts to get noticed. . . .

Cas Walker's "Farm and Home Show" went off the air in 1983 and few East Tennesseans noticed. The show was mourned in places like Washington, D.C., where bluegrass musicians consider it legendary. Performers like the Johnson Mountain Boys thought it an honor to appear on a show where the careers of so many greats began.

★ Bradley Reeves

Back in the late '70s, videotape became more prominent. So they started videotaping Cas. For several reasons—one is because he was getting everybody in so much trouble with his comments, lawsuit potential and what have you. So, "We're gonna pre-tape you and then we're gonna air you at 5:30 in the morning."

The producer, the director of that show, Hal Watson, compiled for his own personal enjoyment a party tape of Cas Walker bloopers and just fantastical, absolutely out-of-this-world, bizarre clips from his television show. There's 30 minutes of it, and it circulated around town for decades in very grainy, washed-out, colorless, awful, hard-to-see copies. We finally found what looks to be a first-generation videotape, and it is clear as a bell. You will not laugh as hard as you will ever laugh while watching 30 minutes—

He makes comments about rubbers and Coke bottles and Dolly Parton's breasts. There's no holds barred. It's television as it was—it was the end of an era, live TV and local TV. Things changed rapidly by the early' 80s. A lot of those local shows went away, and things became more of a national-based entertainment.

And Cas, of course, was a casualty of that.

★ *Knoxville News-Sentinel*, c. 1983

"[Cas Walker's Show] Ends After 35 Years—
Victim of News" by Ken Mink

Cas Walker has been in the news in Knoxville perhaps more than any other person in the city's history as mayor, councilman and civic and governmental official, but now he has become a sort of victim of news.

His early-morning TV show on WBIR-TV, channel 10, is no longer on the air, being bumped to make way for an expansion of the CBS-TV network news. He had been on the air since the station started (Aug. 21, 1956), advertising his chain of grocery stores and introducing up and coming country music stars. His radio shows date back even many years further.

"Knocking me off the air like that means people will wake up and it will be like there's no more Christmas," says Cas. "I sure didn't want to leave, but they told me they wanted to put more network news into that time period."

The show began as Cas Walker's Farm and Home Hour and retained that name over the years even though the show in recent times has only been a half-hour from 6–6:30 a.m.

"I didn't mind so much getting cut back to a half-hour, because I'm getting older. I'm still stout and work 16 to 17 hours a day, but I don't think as fast as I used to." Cas is now 80.

Walker is not bitter about losing the show, though he is disappointed. "My show made money for the station and the ratings were twice as high as the show that followed me," he said. "Another thing—I helped that station get licensed in the first place. Many years ago I traveled on a plane all night to Florida to talk to Congressman Carroll Reece to get his help in approving the license. That was the highest hotel bill I ever paid down there, then or since—a hundred dollars a night."

Walker said he is ready to direct more of his advertising towards newspapers now anyway. "The most recent surveys show that price advertising is most effective in newspapers than anything else."

Over the years Walker has had dozens of entertainers on his show that have gone on to bigger things nationally.

One of his most famous luminaries was Dolly Parton, who began singing on his show when she was only 10 years old. During the last few weeks of Cas' shows, he ran some old tapes showing Dolly performing on his show.

"She was a good 'un, all right. She got better 'n better every week."

Others who were helped in getting their start on Cas' show included such famed personalities as the Osborne Brothers, the Louvin Brothers, Carl Smith, and longtime Grand Ole Opry emcee Ralph Emery.

"I remember I found the first Louvin boy shining shoes in Knoxville and found out he could sing. Then we got together and hunted his brother to put 'em together on the show."

Cas said that as some of his frequent guests became more famous they wound up helping him, too. "I helped 'em get started, but then when they got so well-known, it helped me, too."

One star who he discouraged from continuing her career was Loretta Lynn.

"I told her she had a lot of talent, but that she would never amount to anything because she had a bunch of kids dragging after her. She must've had a half dozen younguns with her all the time. Boy, I sure was wrong, wasn't I?"

Eastside cleanup, February 22, 1981. Printed by permission of the *Knoxville News Sentinel*.

CHAPTER 6

"Cash" Walker, Benefactor

For much of his life, Cas Walker worked to serve the Knoxville community. Yet people have questioned his motivations. Did he act as a benefactor to attract customers, secure votes, or fulfill his Christian duty? No matter the answer, stories abound regarding his generosity, and for many poor people, white and black, he served as a safety net. Since Cas located many of his stores in some of the city's poorer communities, many of the people he helped were also his customers. This chapter reveals the various ways Cas helped people, whether it be through the *Knoxville Journal*'s "Milk Fund," paying for funerals, or offering jobs to ex-convicts. Not only did Cas reach out to the needy, but they also reached out to him by letter. Very often Cas responded in kind.

"A Friend to the Common Man"

★ James Bragg

I think he wanted to be a friend to the common man. I think that's true. I think that he wanted to relate to the everyday Knoxvillian because if he related to them, they'd buy groceries from him. "I'm one of you guys. I'm not some fancy guy, I'm not an out of town guy like this guy that owned the White Store. I'm not Kroger, I'm not A&P, that's owned. Your money stays in here."

And he gave a lot of money away. He gave millions of dollars away. He owned wings at the hospitals. There's a big wing at Fort Sanders that's Cas Walker.

★ Bob Booker

It had to be somewhere about 1945–46, the first time when I really zeroed in on the name Cas Walker. My great grandmother went to church that Sunday, and she came home and she was very excited. "Mr. 'Cash' Walker was at church today."

And of course, what happened—when my great grandmother went, she put a quarter in the collection plate—that's what she had to contribute to church. But she was excited as Mr. "Cash" Walker had put $5 in the plate. And that was an astronomical thing to have happened in that church down on Campbell Avenue.

But Cas was very much into that, because every black person who died—I don't know if he did this in the white community or not—but for every black person who died, Cas would send a plant to the funeral. And with the Cas Walker name and all that kind of stuff on it.

I think Cas generally wanted to help people, and I think he did. But at the same time, it made him a multimillionaire to be involved in these poorer communities. So, I don't think ill of him for that—he was a genius businessman. He did whatever it took to make his money.

★ David West

Me and him would go to church. He said, "My wife's not the same religion, my wife's not the same politics—but we're still married, we love each other! It's not about what you do and who you are."

This is one of the greatest things I learned from Mr. Cas Walker back when I worked with him. I was at church with him one night. We were sitting on the front row. At the beginning of the service, the preacher said, "We've got two people with us now we want to honor and thank them for being here, Cas Walker and David West."

We got a big hand. Then he said, "Mr. Walker, would you like to say something?"

Cas said, "Yeah, I would." He always liked to make a speech.

He stood up—most people stood up and talked from the bench, but when they asked him that, he got up and walked to the microphone. He liked microphones.

On the way up there, the preacher said, "We've got Cas Walker, he's gonna come up here and speak a little bit. The Lord has been good to you, hasn't he, Mr. Walker?"

He said, "Yeah, he has. But I've been good to the Lord, too."

Well, the whole church laughed, and he explained it to them. You could hear a pin drop. He said, "The way you're good to the Lord is from the Bible: 'You saw me hungry, you didn't feed me. You saw me thirsty, you didn't give me no drink. Sick and in prison, you didn't visit me. When did we see you like this, Lord?'"

He said, "I've done it to the least of these back here. Now, if you don't do something for people, and you don't help somebody, and you don't do something, you're not doing anything for the Lord, and don't expect him to do good to you."

The next day, we're going to maybe Virginia after that. He's sitting there, he said, "You know, they didn't understand me much at church last night, at first, did they?"

I said, "What are you talking about, Mr. Walker?" I knew what he was talking about.

He said, "Well, everybody laughed when I said I've been good to the Lord, but David, if you're not good to somebody and you don't help people, he's not gonna do nothing for you."

★ Becky Orange Dwarshuis

Before Cas got into the grocery business, he lived in a boarding house in Maryville. And there was a black gentleman there who had been in an accident, and he had the tips of his fingers sliced so badly that they needed to be amputated, but he didn't go have them amputated. The doctor gave him some salve and Cas Walker said it looked like coal dust and lard mixed together.

Do you know what farmers did with coal ash? Ash and lard? When a male calf was castrated, they would mix up lard and ashes and put it in the incision.

Cas said, "I don't know what it was, but the man had some that the doctor had given him." The fingers were all bandaged, and Cas said no one was talkin' to him or helpin' him. He said the man was runnin' a real high fever, you could just place your hand close to him and feel the heat. And he was delirious sometimes and nobody was helping him, and the man was too sick to bandage his own fingers.

So Cas said, "Every night when I came in, I would take the bandage off and I'd smear that salve in there, then I'd wrap 'em back up, and every morning I would do the same thing."

He said it had a terrible odor, it smelled like rotting flesh. And one day he just removed the bandages and the tips of his fingers—which were decayed—came off, and he said, "Then I could really put that salve on there," and he'd bandage it.

Later Cas Walker left his boarding house. So one time, his driver was takin' him down to Georgia, a car full of men. They were flying in one of those old big cars goin' 100 MPH. And he said a highway patrolman pulled them over, and Cas noticed, as he got out of the patrol car, he was a black man. And he said, "I wanna see your driver's license."

So the driver started gettin' his billfold and Cas said, "I noticed the three tips of his fingers had been amputated," and he said, "I just leaned over and looked and I said [*in imitation Cas-Walker voice*], 'My name's Cas Walker.'"

And the gentleman said, "Cas Walker, I have always wanted to meet you again. You saved my life. Literally I was too sick to bandage my own fingers." And he said, "I couldn't, I was delirious."

And all the men around said, "You have Cas Walker to thank for that!"

★ Ben Walker

I want to tell something positive about Cas. I've heard a lot of criticizin' about him all my life, and I criticized him myself. But when I was eighteen or nineteen—it was either 1957 or 1956—I lived in Blount County, so he gave me a job—which, I wish he hadn't because I worked myself to death—but during the summertime, when I was outta school I worked for him at his Broadway store. So Cas helped people that were, not on the lower end, but down in the *valley*. He helped people who had nowhere else to turn. And this example is what I remember—one of the stories I remember.

I was workin' at Cas Walker's store. So he called out there one day, and he told my cousin—I worked for my cousin, Carl Walker—and he called out there one day and he told Carl to send me and three more guys to the funeral home, that there was a guy out there that had got killed in prison, and the woman, the mother, did not have anybody—and really she didn't.

When we got there, she was the only one there. We went out there—and I was eighteen and I've never forgotten the boy. He was a little guy, looked like a kid. And he had been beaten to smithereens—whether it was by other prisoners, I don't know, or the guards, or what—but he had been killed in prison. Well, this poor woman, she had nobody else to turn to except Cas. So I know that she called Cas and asked him if he could help her. And he sent us out there to be pallbearers.

And I've never forgotten that guy, because it was horrible to me . . . and I hadn't seen many dead people back then anyway. But that is one thing that people don't know about Cas, he did help people who had nowhere else to turn.

Now can you see that woman calling one of the other councilmen and asking them to help her? No—she called *him* to help her.

★ Diana Hawk

I was a senior in Young High School, and seventeen years old. I was campaigning for Homecoming Queen, which was determined by how much money you raised for the athletic department. In addition to the students' donations, I could solicit from anyone. Since I did not drive, a dear friend of mine drove me around to different businesses to request support for me and for the athletic department. I played the accordion for many functions in the area at that time, including the "Midday Merry Go Round" with Lowell Blanchard, who had a regular show on the radio. Cas Walker had a weekly television show on WBIR, so I decided I would sit in the lobby until he came in for his weekly show. I planned to make a deal with him for a donation.

Being the character he was known to be, I knew he would prefer a deal rather than to just ask for money support. When he arrived at the station I jumped up and addressed him. I told him that if he would donate to a worthy cause and for my support to become Homecoming Queen, I would play my accordion on his show.

He agreed and told me what time to be there the next week. I had no interview prior to the show. I was standing off camera, ready to play my accordion and I heard him introducing me as the girl who made a deal with him, which seemed to have pleased him. I played live on his show and was told I would receive his donation in the mail. I was so excited I could hardly wait to receive a donation from Cas Walker that would put me over the top and in first place.

I received an envelope in the mail with a $5.00 bill in it. I have to smile when I think of that experience.

★ Carl Warner

Well, Cas knew of me because I was on television in Knoxville and doing many television broadcasts and producing television news. For a short time, I decided that I wanted to teach, and I was teaching at an all-black high school in Knoxville.

It was rough because the black principal said, "Don't teach them. Just keep them quiet. They're too dumb to learn. We just pass them." And I determined that I was gonna be a teacher, that I would see if I could get the students to pay attention and learn. I was teaching English and civics and home room.

But anyway, I went to my civics class, and it came with a great big mahogany board with little brass plaques on it and they said, "What's that?"

I said, "This is an honor roll plaque. Anyone that makes a C in my class is gonna get a surprise."

"Oh well, what's the surprise?"

I brought with me from my bank a fist full of money, dollar bills and ten-dollar bills, five-dollar bills, even a few hundred-dollar bills. I said, "Well, money like this! And I pulled it out of my pocket and their eyes opened wide open. I said, "Not only will you get this money, but you'll also get a big surprise."

"Well, what's the surprise?"

"Well, listen guys, if I told you the surprise, it wouldn't be a surprise. But the only people who get to know about it are the people who make a C and get on the honor roll."

Anyway, to make a long story short, I thought three or four might make it. Well, I had a class of thirty-two students—*twenty-seven* made C's. If only three or four made it, I had a station wagon and I could take them with my wife and we could enjoy time together, but not for that many!

So I went to Cas and I said, "Cas I'm an idiot, I made a deal with my class. I had no idea that"—and I explained what had happened.

He said, "What's it gonna cost you?"

I said, "To hire a bus and a bus driver and to pay for their overnight stay at the Holiday Inn and to buy their food and to buy them the admission to the big theme park up there, it's gonna cost about $2,800."

He turns to his secretary and he says, "Edna, give Carl a check for $3,000."

That's how I met him.

★ David West

This girl had went out with a cop in Sevierville. She went out with a cop, and the cop paid her $200—he wrote her a check. She took it to Cas Walker's Sevierville store to cash it, but the cop stopped payment on it so it bounced. She didn't have no money.

She done exactly the right thing: be honest. She came to Mr. Walker; she said, "Mr. Walker, I want to tell you the truth about something. I went out with this cop"—told him who it was—"and he paid me $200." She said, "It's not a good thing to do, but I'm broke and I needed some money. He stopped payment on the check now I'm coming to pick it up."

He said, "You don't worry about that, honey. I'd rather see you making some money as a bum." He said, "I'll collect it for you, you don't worry about it. I'll take care of it."

The very next morning, I'm right there, picking for him, banjo around my neck.

[Cas says,] "We got a fellow in Sevierville—I won't call his name but he drives a car with a light going out on top, he's got a badge and a gun. And he went out with this girl and he gave her $200—what for I don't know. Don't make a difference. He wrote her a check, and she's in tears, and he stopped payment on the check. He said that the merchandise wasn't worth $200. I'm not judging it, but I'm gonna tell you right now, if he don't get that $200 check in the Sevierville store picked up today, in the morning I'm gonna call his name."

First thing I do next morning when I walk in: "Did you get your check?"

"Oh yeah, he called me as soon as we got off the TV."

It tickled that little girl to death. That was Cas Walker. If you was a crook, you didn't like him.

★ Becky Orange Dwarshuis

One day, Cas went to work. His cashier was crying. She thought Cas would surely fire her, 'cause she was just sobbing. He said in his gruff voice, "What's wrong with you? Why are you crying?" And she said, "Cas, my daughter, about fifteen years old gonna have a baby any minute. She ran away, she moved in with her boyfriend, she's pregnant, she came home. The boyfriend doesn't want the baby, my daughter doesn't want the baby, and, Cas, I don't want the baby. I don't know what I'm gonna do."

So what do you do when someone tells you that?

He said, "I was so upset."

That afternoon a couple came who sung on the Cas Walker Show. My mother and daddy were personal friends with this couple—and again I can't remember their names—but mother and daddy told me this story too. Cas Walker told me, "That afternoon, they came in and they said, 'Cas in that newspaper you've got, you advertise for everything. Will you advertise that we wanna have a baby? We cannot have a baby, nothing works, and we wanna adopt a baby.'"

And Cas said [*in gruff imitation Cas voice*], "You'll have to go the hospital to get it." And so he went up and introduced the mother to the couple and said, "Call them when your daughter has the baby."

So he said, "I have traded coon-dogs and I've traded horses, and I've traded lots of things, and I've sold lots of cans of pinto beans. But the thing I'm most proud of is that I arranged for a couple to get a newborn baby." And he said, "I followed that baby—and they would bring this little girl back to me and I would get to see her toddlin' along, and she was in a happy home."

★ David West

Mr. Walker was selling his books at Walmart. A little lady walked up, and I'll never forget her, she must have been as old as him. Had two little silver teeth, I don't think they were gold, two little silver teeth. She was even trembling, she was a little bony lady. She got up there and she said, "Mr. Walker, do you remember me?"

He said, "Yeah, I remember your face. I can't recall your name." He had a real good memory.

She said, "I came in your store way back when you was running the produce, you was working in the produce, that white apron. I can see you like it was yesterday. That apron, you was doing produce, I asked you would you sell me $10 worth of groceries on credit. You said no. Here's what you told me. You said: 'No. I wouldn't even sell my mother $10 worth of groceries if she came in the door. But I will loan you $10.' You reached in your billfold, and handed me $10. I said, 'Now I'll pay you back first of the month.' You never said nothing."

She said, "I went back first of the month, walked back there where you were at. You were still doing produce. I never forget what you said. I handed you that $10 and said, 'Here's that $10 I owe you.' You said, 'Damn if it ain't!' and stuck in your pocket. That's all you said!"

Wasn't that such a great story? That's a true story, it's not made up.

★ Larry Mathis

Well, I believe Cas could've robbed a bank up in Kentucky and got caught red-handed, and if they had a jury up there, they'd free him because they thought that he couldn't do no wrong.

Now, one thing he would do, if somebody's house burnt, he'd get them back in housekeeping the next day. He'd get on his show and talk about it. He did that because he wanted to help people, but at the same time—he's dead and he can't defend himself, but when you're working around somebody for twelve or thirteen years, and I'm not putting him down—but at the same time, on one side of his brain is to help somebody: "Let's get those people back, they need it." He'd do that. He'd say, "Hey, we need a refrigerator for somebody. Some of you folks up in Corbin, Kentucky, some of you got an extra refrigerator, you take it over there to them."

But at the same time, we'll say, the Willis family got burnt out. Well, the Willis family, they're not just five people, they've got in-laws and outlaws and when you put them back in housekeeping, them in-laws and outlaws are gonna go to Cas's store and trade with him. So, see, he was doing two good things: He was helping that person out, and he was helping his business out.

You can't blame him for that.

★ David West

And this guy told me—I remember as a kid when this was happening, because I knew some of the people that worked on it—this fellow had a burn-out and they built him a new little two- or three-room house in one day. Cas got on the radio, and he said, "Now we're gonna build these people a house."

This was back before inside plumbing or anything, way back there.

"We're gonna build them a house, we're gonna build it Saturday. I want every available carpenter. I want Shodd Lumber Company, I'll bring you a list today and I want it laying there, most of it precut. And Schubert, here's what you need to bring: windows and doors. Here's what somebody else needs to bring. And I'm gonna advertise for you on TV so you're gonna get plenty of advertisement. You put your signs up there if you want to, but I want that loaded there Friday, because Saturday we're gonna be there at daylight and I want every carpenter. I'm gonna send my boys. I don't care if you can't do nothing but carry lumber, I want you there!"

This man said they built a little three-room house in one day, and even laid the chimney for them. In one day, by dark. Now that's working, ain't it?

"Dear Mr. Walker"

★ Letters from "Broadcast Collection, 1950s," McClung Collection, ETHC

June 21, 1953

Dear Mr. Walker,

This is our first time to ever write to you, but just to get to the facts about this problem. I know you have helped other people such as this man who have needed help and some who didn't need the help as much as they pretended to need it. This man (Mr. Walter Hammond) he is a friend of ours we have known him for 18 years. Why did the city burn down his house? After all he is paralized in his left side. At 60 years of age, a man can't or shouldn't have to live out in an opened field. If we were in his place would we want to live that way? I think the man should have another house built even if its only another one room house. If you decide to do any thing about it, I'm not working regular but I will gladly contribute to a donation to help build another place for him to call his "home."

"A friend"

June 26, 1953
Personal
Mohawk Jenn

Dear Mr. Walker,

I have a favor to ask of you & I hope you can do it for me. I guess you read in the paper's about a man shooting and killing my husband the 2nd of April '53. Some said you were telling about it over the air. We sued this man's wife for $25,000 but at the time they were supposed to have the trial which was the 15th of this month they had it put off because the lawyer said that we were supposed to have waited 6 months before we done anything about suing them & he said the law just required a year to do it in & that if it wasn't done in a year's time that we couldn't do anything else about it. The lawyer we have said that we were allowed to sue them for $25,000 but no more. We just have about 6 months to do this in before the year is up. This man's wife is worth the $25,000, she has a fine home & over a hundred acre's of land and cattle. We live up in a hollow and they own some land between ours and the main road & they were to selfish to give us a road they have. We have a lot of timber on our land but can't sell it because we don't have a road and we can't get food in to our cows & mule.

This trial is to be tried at Morristown but the lawyer we have isn't doing such a good job at it, in fact I think he has been bought off. I have 2 girls age 12 & 15 which has to walk about a mile to catch the school bus.

Here's what I would like for you to do for me?

I would like for you to find me the best lawyer you know of in Knoxville, one that won't sell out. Because all of the lawyers in Morristown is for Williams because they have a little more money than us.

If you can find me a lawyer please let me know where I can get in touch with him at. I am enclosing a stamped self address envelope for your reply.

Sincerely,
Miss John J
Mohawk Jenn
Route #2
Please answer as soon as possible

May 4, 1954
Mtn. City Georgia

Dear Mr Walker,

I'll write you a few lines to say I hear your radio program every day. I think they are the best on the radio. Mr. Walker I'm in very bad need of some help and I am writing to see if I could get any help from you. I am a widow with four babies. I owe a hospital bill of $291. My little home is standing good for the bill. I am not able to work. The welfare wont help me so I'll lose my place the first of June if I don't have the money. I don't have any of my family to turn to for help so what will we do? The doctors said I would be able to work in a little while. So if I could borrow this from you till I go to work I would pay it all back. So please Mr. Walker could or will you help me to keep my home. Don't call names or read this letter over the air.

I'll be waiting for an answer real soon.
   Yours Truly,
   Mrs. Lula M. Bingham
Please do not broadcast my name.

June 7, 1954

Dear Mr. Walker,
   I want you to read this over the radio for me. I am a poor woman and I need help from the good people and I have 5 children. And my first boy is 7 years old and my auther boy is 5 years old and my little girl is 4 years old. And my auther little girl is 4 years old. And my little Baby boy is 1 year old. Now. Please read this on the air for my little kids they need some things to wear. I can't take them to church on Sunday now. Mr. Walker if you can please try and get me some help. And if they have any thing for me why I wear about 18 or 16 size now. The good lord will bless people that help the poor. Now, Mr. Walker, you be sure and read this over the air for I am a poor woman and I have got five little kids. Now give my address to the people so they can send them things to me.
   Mrs. Hattie Gelliam
   Rogersville, Tenn.

Jan 24, 1956

Dear Mr. Walker,
   I have listened [to] your radio programs for the past 5 or so years since we have had a radio. And I know you help a lot of people when you can and would like for you to help me if you can at all.
   I don't know how to start but I will try to tell you the best I can in this letter. I want to ask you first not to read this over the radio. It is about my Mother. She is a very sick person. Her left side is paralized and she can't use it. She can walk a little but not too good. She hasn't been out of the house for about 6 months. When she does get out her leg gives out on her and she falls. She is a heavy built woman and she can't get up when she falls. She needs to be [doctored] but she doesn't have a penny of money coming in from any where and me and my husband don't have the money . . . to take her to the Dr. She really needs in a hospital because I am under the Dr. all of the time and I am not really able to take care of her like she should be taken care of. The reason I am telling you this is I wanted to know if you

knew of a place where they keep old people that don't have any money . . . and look after them like they should be waited on, a place where they really take care of them and don't miss treat them. I wouldn't want her mistreated for anything in the world. If I was able to take care of her I wouldn't think of doing anything like this. . . .

The reason I asked for your help is I thought maybe you knew of a place like I am talking about. She has got to have something done or she is going to die. She can't do a thing for herself but feed herself and can't do that very good. Mr. Walker I believe you will help me if you possible can. I would like for you to even come to see her and see what kind of shape she is in for your self. If you know of a hospital or anything where they take care of people like my Mother would you help me get her in a hospital. She has some kind of spells and I believe if she was in a hospital they could help her about them too. I am the only one in the family that will wait on her. I have a sister but she won't keep her. I have taken care of her since my father died 10 years ago. I wasn't 10 at the time. Of course she didn't get so bad until about 6 years ago. If you can help me I sure would appreciate it. . . .

Well Mr Walker I have told you about all I can explain in a letter. So if you can help me you can let me know as soon as you can. I sure will thank you and I never will forget you.

Yours truly,
A Friend
Mrs. Squire Sharp
Luttrell, Route 2, Tenn.

December 8, 1957

Mr. Cas Walker,

I just want to try to explain to you a few words about the woman that come over to WIVK yeasterday and talked to you for help. She is a good little Christen woman and a mother with 7 children she has 4 deaf children out here in Knoxville school and a husband with one arm he was a coal miner for about 19 year that is where he lost his arm. She is 56 year old and he has been out of a job for a year now and Mr. Walker they are nice honest people and the woman is not just one of those women that goes around begging for help. It is just one of those hard times that comes on some of our good people. Mr Walker she was hurt very bad after talking to you. She depended on you so much. We all told her you was a man with a big hart and a lot of sympathy for people in kneed and Mr Walker you didn't only hurt this little woman but you hurt some of your friends that beleaved in you so much. I am not writing you this letter just to be smart in any way but just to try to tell you these people are really in kneed and you have helped others and good people like this woman and her family is the kind we should help. She is still trying to fine work. They want to try to get moved over here in Knoxville before their children comes home for Christmas the ones that is out here in the Deaf school. . . . Her husband is a good driver and can do a lot of work. . . . He is a good man and is againce whiskey. They are both Christen people and we would be glad to have them down here in Knoxville. We feel they could be some help to this city of Knoxville. We kneed all the help we can get to help this place to be stronger and build up the weak parts. I love good old Knoxville and I love good people that is what makes us happy. So I will close for now as I have just wrote my feelings.

    Yours truly,

    Mrs. John Cupp

PS Mr Walker I do not mean to impose on you but we want to help these people to get moved down here.

December 11, 1957
Knoxville, Tenn

Dear Mr. Walker,

    Am writing these few lines asking you in the name of God wont you please help me my little son who is just 15. He can't get a job be cose he is just 15. He is willing to work. I am to. Ever where I go ask for a job this is what I get. How old are you. I tell them they say I am to old. I am 57. My lights water are off. Mr Walker if I could only get them on. I could make a little ironing washing in my home. Thanksgiving we didn't have a thing to eat. Havent anything now. Wish you could come see. Burning my rugs to keep fire. Mr Walker when my son was living I had a fire and plenty to eat. Mr Walker God must have led me to write to you. I cryed all night amos . . . this is an unfriendly world. No one cares for you. I haven't close to go to church. Wish you could just come out see the home. I am telling the truth, God how it is. Called the well fare they turned us down. Wont you please help us. Mr Walker wont you please help me get my lights water back on.

    I am Miss Blanch M. Thomas, 1106 West Fifth Avenue

    May God Bless you is my prayer.

January 29, 1959

Dear Mr. Walker,

You have helped many people when they needed help and I wonder if you could help me. Here is my problem and I do hope you can help me out. My name is Don Hurst and I am 25 years old. When I was 20 I got into some trouble and was sent to prison for 10 years. I made a good record when I was in and I was released November 28, 1958 on parole, after I served a little over five years. I am to stay on parole till November 20, 1959. After I came out I had a job working in a furniture store but the owner ... said he was going out of business after Saturday, January 26. So, I will be out of a job and I will face to go back to prison if I can't get a job. I have met a nice girl since I came out and I plan to marry her about June. This is the first time in my life that I feel something to live for. Mr. Walker if you can get me any kind of job, I'll take it and be very thankful. I made a mistake once but now I want to make up for it. Mr. Walker, the things I wrote on this paper is true and I have not lied to get you to help me.

"He Had to Watch Everything and He Was Smart"

★ David West

He let everybody in. We were live on the show for an hour and a half. We went on at 5:30–7:00. I opened it up for nine years. If you walked in to the television station and stood there, maybe nobody spoke to you. In a minute, when Mr. Walker took a break, he'd walk up and say, "Was you needing something?"

People would come to him—he had to watch everything and he was smart. He was concerned about people. He built houses, he did good deeds, and if you was a crook—and he told me, I'm driving with him, I drove him every few days, no cellphones, we could talk for six hours. He said, "Now, I have to be real careful about people coming on TV advertising for a burnout or somebody needing help, because they gather up a lot of stuff and they go to the flea market with it."

He had you checked. Believe me, he had eyes in the back of his head, so don't never try to pull nothing. That's the reason he liked me, 'cause I was 100 percent.

Ginny and the Milk Fund

★ *Knoxville Journal,* December 18, 1990

"Milk Fund Supporter, Cas Walker, Comes Back Home" by Betty Bean

It was a bittersweet homecoming Monday for Cas Walker. The "Old Coonhunter" left the Blount County nursing home where he'd been for four years to take up residence in the house on Gaston Avenue where he and his wife, Ginny, lived for so long.

There's a flash of his old feistiness when he brags about how far he's come since the time four years ago when he was written off as hopelessly addled.

"They tried to say I have Alzheimer's," he said. "That's what some were telling. . . . But they've done me a world of good here, and I'm getting to where I walk a right smart every day. I'll come back and visit them."

A sliver of dread pokes through when he talks about facing Christmas alone. "I lost Ginny, you know. She died at 5 minutes to 7 on Saturday morning, Nov. 3. If she'd lived till the next day we'd have lived together 62 years. . . . Ginny always put up a good Christmas tree, but I don't think I want one now. She planned for Christmas, you see. . . . She always cooked a good meal, and they'd all come home. . . . I miss my wife, you know. It'll be an awful hard Christmas without her."

. . . Walker wasn't up to being actively involved in the 1990 Journal Milk Fund campaign. Virginia Walker's death last month took too much out of him. But he's still concerned, and fears that coming hard times will strain the fund unless collections are good this season.

"The last few years, we haven't had many bad winters. But this year we'll be having lots more bad weather and it'll put people out of work. They's an awful lot of roofers, painters, and construction workers that won't be able to work," Walker said. "And I want people to help the best they can. I'm as much for the Milk Fund as I ever was, but there's been so much a'happening with my wife sick and all."

Ginny Walker always used to help with Milk Fund collections, he said. And collecting more money than her famous husband got to be a game with her. "Ginny liked competition," he said. "She'd visit people she knew, places where she traded, and she'd try to beat me. One time, she went to Wolfe Dairies, a place that'd always give me about $800, and got them to give me $400 and her $400. There was people that'd give to her that wouldn't give to me."

Walker smiles when he reminisces about meeting Virginia Grantham, a girl with reddish brown hair so long she could sit on it and a father who wouldn't let her date. It was 1923, and Walker, newly returned from working in the Kentucky coal mines, had opened a grocery store on Vine Avenue with Bob Loveday. They sold groceries to the Grantham family in South Knoxville, and Walker delivered the goods in a wagon drawn by a pony who knew every customer on the route.

"Ginny had beautiful hair," Walker said. "After we were married, she got to wanting to cut it off, and I told her I'd divorce her if she cut her hair. So she cut her hair off and she wanted to know if I'd divorce her."

During their long marriage, Virginia Walker helped him in the business, and helped serve as a kind of moral compass for him, too. She taught a Sunday school class for years and kept a close eye on her flamboyant husband, who was a leader in Knoxville politics for more than 30 years.

He says he plans to live in the Gaston Avenue house with the licensed practical nurse who cared for Ginny. The place will be empty, now, though. His only child, daughter Wilma June, died years ago. One of her sons, Buster Roberts, was raised by Cas and Ginny Walker, and he was killed two years ago.

The Walkers also raised a nephew, Odell Cas Lane, who worked with Walker in the grocery store business and was a state legislator for 14 years. "He had cancer," Walker said. "And when he died, it hurt me almost as bad as when Wilma June did. The two of them was raised together, you see."

The Milk Fund is administered at no cost by the General Assistance Office at the Knox County Welfare Department, and every cent collected goes toward good purchases. Last year's drive brought in $76,469. Sponsors are The Journal, WIVK, WKXT-TV, Weigel's, the Bistro, the Knox County Sheriff's Department and the Knoxville Teen Board.

Before the City Council fistfight between Cas Walker and J. S. Cooper, March 1956. Printed by permission of the McClung Collections, East Tennessee History Center.

CHAPTER 7

Bare-Knuckle Politics

Cas Walker's formal political career began in 1941. His years in the grocery business meant many knew the man as a local proprietor and community leader, and his later years as a media mastermind would further solidify his public presence. Some of the most outlandish stories about Walker come from his thirty years as a local politician. As Cas often did, he made the best of certain situations and spun even his worst moments into stories that cast him in a positive light. One of the main tenets in his life was that there was "no such thing as bad publicity." In fact, the one photograph that solidified Cas's "bare-knuckle" reputation appeared in the 1950s when he attempted to punch a fellow councilman, which *Life* magazine published. This chapter describes many elements of Cas's political career in the words of local Knoxvillians.

Councilman and Mayor

★ *Metro Pulse*, July 30, 1998, by Betty Bean (Excerpt)

Walker ran for City Council in 1939 and was narrowly defeated. Undeterred, he won a seat in 1941, and by the time he was elected mayor in 1945, he owned seven retail stores, two feed stores, a wholesale grocery, a stockyard and a dairy. He was strong in the inner-city black and poor white wards, where he commenced to grow larger than life and ornerier than a whole trainload of SOBs.

O. C. Johnson, known as "Little Cas" during the 25 years he ran Walker's C&R green stamp operation, summarizes Walker's entree into Knoxville this way: "Victor Ashe come riding in on his Mam's apron strings. That old man (Walker) dug his way in the coal mines of Kentucky and in a little old square box store on Vine Street."

In 1928, he married Virginia Grantham, a pretty Knoxville girl with red hair so long she could sit on it. He says he "went pig wild over her" from the very beginning. They had one daughter, Wilma June, born in 1930.

A letter to the editor of the Knoxville Journal in 1943 asked: "Do we want a mayor who by his own admission has amassed a fortune yet tries to make the lower-income citizens believe that every man with an extra pair of socks is a predatory capitalist who spends most of his time devising means to suck lifeblood out of the working people?"

Walker was elected mayor in 1945, by virtue of being the leading vote-getter among the Council candidates. He entered office with an agenda, telling a Journal reporter election night that his first order of business would be "a good businessman being city manager."

This was a shot across the bow of City Manager George Dempster, whom Walker charged with "being too dominant at Council meetings. I favor letting the Council run the city for change. . . ." Dempster resigned before Walker could fire him.

There's a chapter in Walker's autobiography entitled "No Other Mayor In The City Of Knoxville Has Ever Found Stolen Merchandise Or Lowered The City Tax Rate, Except For Me." It fails to mention the fact that he was recalled.

[Historians Bruce] Wheeler and [Michael] McDonald's *Knoxville, Tennessee* summarizes Mayor Walker's troubles thusly: "Now he was mayor and no longer able to talk with impunity and conviction about being an outsider. He was obliged to take care of his supporters, many of whom hungered for city offices . . . Now he had to try to solve such thorny issues as taxes, the city's bonded indebtedness zoning and unemployment."

Walker's hand-picked city manager lasted only 11 weeks in office before Walker led a move to fire him. An irate business elite forced a recall vote and ran a lumber company executive against him in a December election that Wheeler and McDonald call the dirtiest in Knoxville's modern history.

Walker was cast out of office, but the silk-stocking crowd had little time to celebrate. Within 10 months, he was back on the Council, once again the leading vote-getter. He reclaimed his place as the resident "aginner," opposing sales tax referendums, consolidated government, construction of a City/County building, construction of the Civic Auditorium and fluoridated water, which he believed was communistic.

O. C. Johnson remembers an advertisement taken by Walker's political opponents: "Squawk, Cas, Squawk. How would you like to live in Squawkerville?"

In 1956, a photograph of Walker slugging a City Council colleague made Life Magazine (although he would admit, years later, that the fight was a publicity stunt). He gloried in his uncouth image, which couldn't have been more offensive to the Chamber of Commerce bunch [than] if he'd driven by Cherokee Country Club and flipped them the finger.

McDonald and Wheeler describe Walker during this era as an elemental force in politics: "blunt, acerbic, tough and eternal, he could deliver 20,000 votes on any issue on a given day."

He ended the decade with a successful battle to defeat a referendum to consolidate the city and county. He was still prospering financially into the early '60s, but later that decade, his political base started showing signs of decay. Although he continued to be elected, he was no longer a front-runner, and began to be mocked more than feared.

McDonald and Wheeler: "The savage warrior, who made no money personally from his years in local government but who had been generous with jobs and other favors to political friends, saw the handwriting on the wall. In the eyes of the newcomers he simply had to be eliminated."

Cas sworn in as Mayor of
Knoxville, April 17, 1959.
Printed by permission of the
Knoxville News Sentinel.

Nicknames for Cas's Enemies

★ Bo Pierce

Cas had a penchant for giving opponents nicknames and politicians through the years; national politicians do the same, even now. But Cadillac Jack Cooper, one of his nemeses on city council—labeling him "Cadillac Jack" just puts in the minds of Cas's followers that this guy's a little uppity, he's a part of the "silk stocking crowd," which was another phrase that Cas liked to employ.

★ Bruce Wheeler

He always referred to his competitors as the "silk stocking crowd." He told these great political stories and he always had nicknames for all his rivals—there was a fellow who worked for the county, and he found out that this guy had had a fence put around his property at county expense, and there were posts in the ground and then I guess wire fencing. So his nickname was "Post-Hole" Toby Julian. There was a fellow who had the popcorn concession at the Chilhowee Park and he was "Popcorn Cooper."

At the same time, he could make deals with these people to either get what he wanted or trade.

No Such Thing as Bad Press

★ Jack Sharp

TV was young then, not as sophisticated. . . .

I don't know that Cas was trying to sell groceries on his show. In fact, I questioned that myself several times: "Are you out there promoting politics, or are you on there to sell groceries?"

But he saw a blend there that obviously worked. He saw an opportunity to combine, to make people look at his show, to show them—"it's the Sign of the Shears, here you can buy pork chops for this." Cas Walker—Sign of the Shears. You ever heard that one? Sign of the Shears, and he'd have those scissors cuttin'.

People were watching him, and I think he was hoping in the back of their minds: "Well, I'm gonna stop by and get me some of these pork chops."

And I think that when he got by himself—he'd sit down and laugh at people and say, "Got you this time, didn't I? Little old Cas Walker here got *you* this time. You jump on me, I'll jump back at you, 'cause I like it!" It helped his stores, because whether you liked the man or not or approved of him, you knew who Cas Walker was.

He used to say, "Call me anything you want to, do anything to me that you want to, but spell my name right."

Getting the Vote by Any Means Possible

★ Jack Sharp

His office was off Chapman Highway, back behind some stores, on a little street. I remember going over there with some friends of mine, older friends, when I was just a teenager. And he'd have that desk, those big ol' long tables, and four or five women running around behind him and he'd be hollering at them.

I'd sit there and think, "What in the world am I into?" But that's the way he operated.

It was fun just to sit there and watch the different people come in that office to see him. And occasionally you might see somebody that wasn't supposed to be there, an elected official or something like that, that would get hit publicly and just raise the devil about him.

And I'd sit there waiting on him, or waiting on whoever I was with, and I'd think, "What are *you* doing here?"

But they'd come in a side door, they didn't come in the front door. That's what tipped me off to the whole thing. If people knew, they wouldn't believe it. I learned that as a kid.

★ Bob Booker

It was the norm in those days to pass about whiskey. There are newspaper pictures of men sitting around the polls who haven't voted, and they're waiting for the man to bring their half pint and then they would go vote. I remember the first time I voted that happened to me. One of the men who owned the liquor stores that Cas Walker set up—I went to vote and he gave me a little ticket. He said, "Now after you vote"—he told me how to vote—he said, "come back and give me this ticket and I'll give you a dollar."

Of course, I didn't give him the ticket back, because I wanted to vote the way I wanted to vote. I'm twenty-two years old, voting for the first time; you can't tell me how to vote.

So, a lot of that went on. A lot of it.

★ James Bragg

You've probably heard this one, it's been around forever. Cas told me about this one. This was when he was running against [George] Dempster.

He said, "You know how I won that election?"

I said, "No, how'd you win it?"

He said, "What I did was, I rounded up a bunch of little school girls, and I bought them all new dresses. And I put two little school girls at every poll."

You've got all these men out there passing out cards. These little girls are passing out cards that say "vote for Uncle Cas."

"And I went down and got a bunch of drunks, and I gave them a fifth of liquor. I told them to drink it. And I gave them some money. I said, 'You've got liquor and money when you come back.'"

He put two of them out at every poll. "If you get arrested, I'll pay your bail."

He said, "I had them to solicit votes for George Dempster."

It was a landslide. . . .

I remember George Dempster said something, that, "If I ordered a dozen son of a bitches, and they sent me Cas Walker, I'd sign for the order." Something like that.

"Swearing-In Ceremony," by Charlie Daniels. Printed by permission of the *Knoxville News Sentinel.*

★ Bo Pierce

And getting back to political races, he would also—say his candidate's name started with a B, he would scour anybody and stick them in the ballot, get enough names, stick them on the ballot that started with A, wherever on the ballot. If he had an opponent whose name started with a B, he'd go get some A's and whatever to put on there, because a certain number of folks, when they get in that box back in the old days anyway, and flip a switch or poke a card, they ain't gonna sit there if it's a big long list. They're gonna hit the first one they come to. That'd take a vote away from his opponent. Anyway, he would load up the ballot that way.

★ Carl Warner

There were a couple things that were on his absolutely hit list. One: during local elections, he decided that he was gonna put people in office that he wanted, for whatever reason. It was not unusual for him to have a pickup truck full of bags of liquor, cheap liquor, and get all the bums, give them the liquor but not until after they voted, and give them a card showing them how to vote and when they came out, he would give them the liquor.

Then, he was pretty smart—no actually, he was damn smart. But what he did, the earliest voting machines had numbers on the back, and the voting officials would come and look at the machines to be sure all the numbers were 00000 for each candidate. After the vote they had to come and manually look at the numbers at the back of the machine.

Well, he had this idea, he'd put a bright card, when I say a bright card, a heavy card with this bright surface, and he would put numbers on it, and set them with a monofilament line, and the numbers all read 000. But the machine would be preprogrammed for votes for his candidate as much as 100 or 200 votes.

The voting officials didn't see it because there was a card in there showing 000, and then when the election started, he had paid people to pull those cards out, and the voting officials didn't look at the numbers again until the end of the day, and they recorded them on their pads.

So, very often, whoever he wanted to win in the local elections, they won. It was a very clever scheme. He showed it to me, so I knew about it.

Mary Pat Tyree, Cas Walker, and Randy Tyree, May 19, 1981.
Printed by permission of the *Knoxville News Sentinel*.

Cas and the Youngest Mayor Ever Elected in Knoxville

★ Randy Tyree

Cas was probably at the height of his influence, overall, during the '60s, '70s, and into the '80s. But all the time that I was working in the '60s and '70s, I had ten years of law enforcement. There were so many issues that we were dealing with as a country, and, I was being drawn to public service. Having already served as a policeman, I was sort of drawn to the political arena out of that. Cas would write stories in the *Watchdog*, for whatever reason, we always got along. He would write favorable stories in the *Watchdog* about me because I was a policeman, and he depended on the police an awful lot for protection, so to speak, because of where his stores were, because they were in some pretty tough spots of town.

Moving into the election in '75, leading up into that time, Cas had a penchant for supporting, his words were "on the outside, throwing rocks to the inside." That was his lifestyle and he was good at it. He would always be against the establishment. The Chamber of Commerce was called the "good government bunch." It was sort of like, if you were organized and for something, Cas was going to be "agin' it," in his words. "I'm agin' that!"

What happened, moving into the election of '75, as was his usual case, he was giving Mayor [Kyle] Testerman what for, just critical of this and that. The mayor he had a bunch of, he called them, "the Kiddie Corps." Kyle had some very efficient and good young people in his administration. But they earned the nickname of the "Kiddie Corps" from Cas.

What it came down to was, in retrospect, that I had good name recognition and a good history in the community, by my police work, and my fighting against the drug problem and being honored basically by the work we did on rehab and education, as well as law enforcement.

But anyway, that helped me with the community, in order to have a foundation, but the key to it was, at that time, I was such an underdog, nobody took me seriously.

Bottom line, as it turned out, it was a foregone conclusion that Kyle was going to get a second term. The issue became how badly I was going to get beat. My one great memory was that about two weeks before the election, Jimmy the Greek paid a visit to Knoxville, and he gave the odds for Kyle's reelection, I think it was five-to-one odds in favor of him.

The assumption among the politicians was that Kyle was gonna sweep me out in the primary.

Had it not been for Cas, he would have, because what happened was, there were, at the time, twelve to fourteen what they call "float wards," where you would go in and do what they call "setups" the night before the election. That's when the paper bags came out, with the five bucks, the pints, et cetera. That was just the way business was done.

I knew I was going to get slaughtered in those wards. So, I went to Cas, and I knew he and Kyle had a falling-out, probably within forty-eight hours of when Kyle had gotten elected four years before.

I went out to his home, and I have it clearly in my mind, that Miss Virginia, his wife, Ginnie, answered the door and they obviously knew who I was and they said come in, Cas was sitting in his chair in the living room.

He said, "Welcome in," and immediately got down to business: "What can I do for you? You gon' get beat, ain't ya?"

I remember that I got to stay positive here. I said, "Well, I've got a shot, but I've gotta have your help."

"Well, what can I do?"

I was honest with him. I said, "I'm gonna get killed in these float wards."

He pumped me pretty good, because he didn't want to get connected with a loser, and at that point I was a well-known loser. So, we chatted a few minutes, and he said, "Well, let me think about this. I might be able to help you." He never committed.

I left not having a clue. Well, when the vote came in on primary night, I made the runoff. Well, that blew up everything because all of a sudden, I was viable and credible.

What I found out later was that Cas had always been active in those wards, but he was never out there himself. He used his nephew—nowadays he would've been called a political operative. His nephew was Odell Cas Lane. He was a ward-smith, so to speak, doing the setups, I found out.

In the next two weeks, we generated—it was such a dramatic process, because of being the underdog and getting into the runoff—it generated a huge amount of public interest. It was sort of like the proverbial Goliath deal. I had survived and made myself credible with the political folks. Within that two weeks, there was an additional 10,000 voters that turned out for the runoff election. That runoff election was very close again.

The long and short of it was, what Cas had done on the primary—and he stayed with me two weeks later to do the same thing—but on primary night, the people who were doing the setup of the wards for Kyle went in about 8:00 o'clock at night and they set all the wards up. Odell Cas Lane—and I know this firsthand because it came direct from Cas to me; there was no intermediary—he said, "The way that went down and the way that you did as well as you did, I sent Odell Cas Lane out after midnight, and he reset the wards."

You set a ward, and then if you don't watch your back, and if you don't have operatives out there, it'll get reset on you.

Well, in the primary, Testerman, his administration was so confident, they knew they had the wards set, they didn't bother because they didn't give Cas credit of being a real astute politician. They just didn't see it coming. It was sort of, they didn't watch their backs and they paid the price.

He was such a player that, of all the things that could have kept me from being elected, if Cas had not showed up as he did, I certainly would not have been elected. Because there was so many things—and that's the reason that after that election, I would never ever, and to this day, I will never badmouth Cas. I just have a personal appreciation for him and a respect for him, which is a combination of a lot of different things, but more than anything else, he was a fighter.

The Fistfight and *Life* Magazine

★ Bruce Wheeler

The fistfight at city council, somebody told me that that picture appeared in *Pravda*. I never actually saw the copy, but I've heard that it did, with the cutline "American Democracy in Action" or something,

I think it was "Popcorn" Jimmy Cooper. There was something that Cas had said about "Popcorn" Jimmy Cooper, and Cooper said, "I'll punch you in the face." Cas said something like, "You try it."

Someone who was there told me that not a punch was really ever landed. They threw a lot of punches but never did hit anybody.

★ Bo Pierce

On the famous photo of him getting ready to punch Cadillac Jack at city council meeting: if you look at newspaper accounts back at that time, or the magazine account at that time, no blows were landed. It looks like Cas is getting ready to knock his head off. And I assure you the Cas I knew in the '70s and early '80s was a powerful, powerful man. He still coon-hunted. He'd pull his pants leg up and show you his calf muscle, and I mean, it—he could do squats, I'm sure, of a pretty impressive amount. Back at that time, he was even in better shape, obviously. And I guarantee you he could have cleaned the floor with anybody in that council meeting.

But no blows were landed, and Cas told me one time, he said, "I had that staged. I had the cameraman ready and I told him when I was getting ready to do it, so I could get that picture."

And again, who knows? That's what he said. But he's selling groceries.

The councilmen's fistfight, March 1956. Printed by permission of the McClung Collections, East Tennessee History Center.

★ Betty Bean

The famous story of him punching Councilman Cooper, Cas told me that that was staged. He said it was a put-up job.

If you look at the picture, back in the background, there are two guys just bent over laughing. And that made *Life* magazine I think. I don't know the reason why. But Cas did a lot of things just for attention. Just for notoriety. And he liked the image of himself as a brawler and a he-man.

And that wasn't just an image. He was rough as a cob.

★ Letter from "Broadcast Collection, 1950s," McClung Collection, ETHC

March 9, 1956

Dear Mr. Walker:

The enclosed clipping appeared in a paper in Turkey and my nephew Jimmy Gibson is in the service there and he said he sure got all there is from the U.S.A.

Thought you might like to see it.

Yours truly,
Mrs. Roy Johnson,
Morristown, Tennessee

"I'm Agin' it!"

★ Bruce Wheeler

Walker at one time or another opposed almost every idea to move the town forward, and then afterwards, he said, "Well, I supported that!"

He opposed the city-county building, he opposed the library, he opposed Market Square Mall, he opposed Daylight Savings Time—he opposed all of it! It was almost a joke.

He claimed that water fluoridation was a Communist plot. There were rumors going around—I think this must have been the McCarthy Era—that that's what it was, it was poisoning the water, the idea that our water was impure. Also I think in the early years, I'm guessing that water fluoridation didn't quite taste as good as it does now.

Daylight Savings Time, he opposed that. Now that's just incredible.

★ Bo Pierce

I attended the first board meeting of the new [Knox] County Housing Authority, where I was a housing counselor. It was in the Andrew Johnson Hotel, about March of '77. There were some prominent community people on the board. Cas was late, wasn't there. Five-member board, so there were four there. They had a lady taking minutes, and the chair of the meeting had waited as long as he could, and he said, "Let's go ahead and call the roll."

And you couldn't have scripted it better. As the secretary said, "Mr. Walker," he was walking in the door, and without asking any questions or whatever, as soon as she said, "Mr. Walker," he said, "I'm agin' it!" and come on around and set down.

Some folks were gigglin'. I didn't know what to do, in that position. The chair cleared his throat and said, "Mr. Walker, we're just callin' the roll."

"Well, well . . . OK." [*in imitation gravelly Cas voice*]

And we went on with the meeting. And he's often been called an "aginer," and that was one of the first things I heard out of his mouth, in relation to the Housing Authority—"I'm agin' it!"

★ Randy Tyree

Mayor [Leonard Reid] Rogers had proposed to buy ten gondolas and put them on Chilhowee Lake as a revenue source for people to take gondola rides. I think they were going to cost something like two or three thousand dollars apiece.

Cas, obviously, he was "agin' it." So they went back and forth. It was a budget issue and all the council people were chiming in. Finally, Cas just yelled into the microphone, got everybody's attention; he says, "Now this is just a lot of money and I ain't gonna vote for this." But he said, "It would make a lot more sense to me for these here gondolas we're talking about, why don't we just buy two and breed them?"

So, the council fell apart. It was sort of one of those classic "you had to be there" times, to see what everybody's reaction was. But it was classic Cas.

★ Julia Tucker

Yeah, he was an "aginer." We have him to thank, partially, for the I-40 expressway that's coming right through Knoxville, because he actually believed that if we had all these expressways come right through Knoxville, that people would get off and shop. Well, they don't, they fly right through.

He was against the Civic Coliseum. He wanted the old Knoxville High School to be turned into an auditorium. So, he was "agin'" that. Can't think of what else he was "agin'" but I'm sure it was a long list. And of course, every time consolidation came up with city and county, he was against that because he would just lose some power.

He was driven by the coal mines of Kentucky. To get as far away from that as he could. And to prove to himself that he was more, and better, smarter, and as good as. The man was absolutely driven. I'm surprised that he slept. His mind was, when it was active, it was like sparklers; it was flying in all sorts of directions. And every once in a while, it would land on something that would come back, and he would have a story.

But it was a control issue. And that's what people in power get. They become satiated with control. Little control, big control. It doesn't really matter what it is; it's just that they loved control, and that's the power of politics. It becomes all-empowering around people, and when they find out they have a little control, they believe they can get more control, and unfortunately, many of them can. And if you can't control, you become a puppet master and get people in power that can do your bidding.

★ Randy Tyree

He, for years, opposed the World's Fair. It was sort of like all these crazy things that was going to happen. Thousands of people were gonna come in, and all these vehicles, and smog, et cetera, we were gonna get sort of wiped out as a city, with carbon monoxide. And it had credibility with a lot of people because even over at the university, there was an environmentalist, and this would've been in the late '70s—but he came to city council and made a really good presentation that we were in danger of carbon monoxide poisoning.

Well, Cas had a field day, because here was a university professor—and Cas obviously only reported what he wanted to—but he ran all sorts of

Watchdog articles about all the reasons why the World's Fair was bad for this community.

Well, about three to four months before the fair opened, Cas came out *for* it. He came out for it by explaining—and there was a lot of backwater negotiations going on with the organization, et cetera, because we knew we had to have every conceivable person going for the fair—but Cas was persuaded....

He still was a devil's advocate because he was a disbeliever in the fact that we were gonna get, at that time we were projecting 8 to 9 million (we wound up with over 10 million)—but there was gonna be 8 to 9 million. He said, "I don't believe that. They might possibly get 5 million, on a good day, but I still knew that even if they got 5 million, I was gonna sell a bunch of groceries."

So, it was consistent, looking to the business end of things of how he could best sell groceries, and that's what made him a success.

Politics and Groceries

★ Jack Wiedemann

Well, when I came here WATE was out in an old mayonnaise factory building across from Fisher Tire on Broadway. It had terrible sound in there, they had metal ceilings and metal walls. We took egg flats and stapled them all over so we had decent sound.

Cas already had a show there, and I think one on WBIR as well. The FCC passed a law about equal time. If you start talking politics the other person gets equal time, and Cas was castrating people on the air that he didn't like.

I told him, "You can't do that anymore. If you talk politics, I'll have to cut you off the air."

He said, "Nobody cuts me off the air."

I said, "Well, I'm telling you that's the new law and I'm gonna do it."

He said, "Ha ha ha!" and laughed at me.

He went on his show, and the first thing out of his mouth, he started talking about John Duncan, who I think was running at that time, and started castrating John Duncan, and I cut him off the air.

I said, "You're off the air."

He said, "I'm not."

I said, "Yes, you are." Then I said, "If you want to talk, you talk about something else."

He said OK.

I put him back on the air. He started talking about grocery business, but then he started back on Duncan again and I cut him off the air again.

I just cut his sound and said, "You're off the air again. The Federal Communications Commission has a law, and I'm obeying that law."

He said, "I'll have your damn job."

And the rest of the program he talked about groceries.

The next day, he went down to see my bosses at the downtown office to get me fired. They told me he was coming so I went down there.

He said, "I want you to fire this little smart aleck here. Blah blah blah."

I said, "Mr. Walker?"

"Hmm?" [*a growl, like Cas's voice*]

"I was doing my job. That's all I was doing. I was doing my job."

He said, "Well, it's a hell of a job."

I said, "Yeah, but I like it."

He said, "I guess you're not going to fire him?"

My boss said, "No, he was doing his job."

He [Cas] said, "Well, hell." And then he left.

Cas Walker Band. Printed by permission of the Tennessee Archive of Moving Image and Sound [TAMIS], East Tennessee History Center. No date provided, ca. 1950s–60s.

Cas Walker on the children's bus. Printed by permission of the Tennessee Archive of Moving Image and Sound [TAMIS], East Tennessee History Center. No date provided, ca. 1940s.

Cas's Family. Date unknown. Printed by permission of the *Knoxville News Sentinel*.

Mayor Walker with Orange Bowl Queen, c. 1945.
Printed by permission of the *Knoxville News Sentinel*.

Cas during his tax evasion trial, c. 1961.
Printed by permission of the
Knoxville News Sentinel.

Cas on the court house steps after being acquitted of charges of tax evasion, c. 1961. Printed by permission of the *Knoxville News Sentinel*.

Cas sworn in as councilman, January 1964. Printed by permission of the *Knoxville News Sentinel*. Picture also includes city leaders W. Dwight Kessell, Milton E. Roberts, and Howard N. Kesley.

Cas Walker motions to "Speak up!" Printed by permission of the *Knoxville News Sentinel*.

Fire at Walker's Magnolia Avenue store, c. 1924.
Printed by permission of the *Knoxville News Sentinel*.

Cas Walker on trial, c. 1981.
Printed by permission of the
Knoxville News Sentinel.

Cas Walker, "Straighten," c. 1985. Printed by permission of the *Knoxville News Sentinel*.

Cas Walker's final resting place, Woodlawn Cemetery. September 28, 1998. Printed by permission of the *Knoxville News Sentinel*.

Cas alone in the crowd. Printed by permission of the *Knoxville News Sentinel*.

CHAPTER 8

Cas on Communism and Civil Rights

During the 1950s and 1960s, Americans faced the formidable challenges of a "red scare" over the threat of communism and the civil rights movement's demand for an end to Jim Crow segregation in the South. By this time, Cas had served as a city councilman for years and solidified his place as one of the city's most vocal conservatives and contrarians. Reflecting the complexity of these intertwined issues, Cas waged a media campaign against Communist influence in Knoxville, which he found in the liberal activism of the Highlander Center, and even in the water. But at the same time, he could be more pragmatic and open-minded, supportive of a peaceful resolution to student demands for desegregation. To this day, his legacy and his reputation on these issues remains controversial, and his role in these events reflects the wider history of Knoxville at a crucial turning point in American history—a city that perpetuated the injustices of racial segregation for far too long but, when forced to change, managed the transition more peacefully than did many other southern cities.

Fluoridation: "A Communist Plot"

★ James Bragg

Cas said that fluoride was a Communist plot to kill our children. Dentists that talked to him said, "Cas, this is good solid sense." He wouldn't have any of it.

I went to University of Tennessee in Memphis, in '76. The public health book there we had—he made the book: "Knoxville millionaire grocer Cas Walker says fluoride's bad for children, because it's a Communist plot to kill our children. It's poison."

It *is* poison, but in four parts per billion . . . but he kept it out of Knoxville water until 1971. Can you believe that?

★ Larry Mathis

For Cas, fluoride was like it was arsenic or cyanide. But I can understand that. Nowadays you see, by getting the water out of the river, every stream around here. Used to, when I was growing up, we'd drink out of every creek and branch we came to. Hunting and stuff. Didn't matter.

But now, this little stream right here [*pointing out the window*], it used to furnish water for three houses. There's a spring up here on the hill. But now there's people that live up on that ridge and their septic tank goes right into it. And the pollution that we have now from factories and things. I understand that it's good for your teeth and stuff, but at that time, it was a new thing, and they didn't know whether your ears would fall off in a year or whatever.

Anything like that that you're unsure of, you're probably not gonna vote for it. That's the way Cas was about stuff.

The Highlander Center

★ Bruce Wheeler

The Highlander Center was driven out of Monteagle. So they moved to Knoxville, and they moved up into the Fort Sanders area. Walker sort of joined in with people who said that these were Communists.

No, they probably weren't Communists, they probably were liberals, they probably were reformers, and there was a lot of that going around in that era.

There was a fellow who was a Walker ally, I don't think they were politically allied, and he would go through the garbage at the Highlander Center, looking for stuff. He's also the person, I think he was—I don't know if he was a Presbyterian or a Lutheran—but he broke into his own church and tore the hymn "We Shall Overcome" out of all the hymnbooks.

★ Victor Ashe

The Highlander Center was an easy one, and then he could throw in the notion: "You know, they have that 'free love' thing out there." He'd always refer to it in that vein.

I think the truth is the Highlander Folk Center was people certainly politically left of center. In today's world, they would be liberal, but they weren't Communists; they weren't even Socialists. Fairly harmless. This was not some cell from Moscow that opened up here in East Tennessee. These were people who had much more advanced, much more liberal viewpoints on issues than the average East Tennessean had in those days.

And you forget, in the '50s and '60s, particularly the '50s and the late '40s in the McCarthy era, a real Communist scare, which McCarthy played on until it blew up in his face. And he made utterly false allegations.

But the Highlander Folk Center was sort of the local version of the Red Cell, which it *wasn't*, but was painted out that way. They supported integration at a time when a lot of white people did not, no question about that.

★ *Knoxville News-Sentinel,* January 15, 1967 (Edited)

"Cas Walker, Highlander Mix It Up: FCC Declines to Act on Phone Tape Recording" by Powell Lindsay

WASHINGTON, Jan. 14—A flap between grocer-politician Cas Walker and Knoxville's ultra liberal Highlander Research Center has landed at the door of the Federal Communications Commission. But not for long. The FCC threw it right back to Knoxville and pointed the way to the Tennessee Public Service Commission.

In a letter to the FCC last month, Highlander board member Walter Bishop complained that Walker was behind a move to spread false charges to the public about Highlander through several "dial-a-message" telephone numbers.

Got Copy

"Dial-a-message" is a device whereby a telephone company subscriber leases a telephone number that when dialed, automatically triggers a tape recorded message.

"Since Cas started harassing us a couple of months ago," Bishop told the commission, "Highlander has been fire bombed, shot into and our fire insurance canceled. I doubt seriously that Cas is doing these things personally, but he might be inciting others with false tales like the one about a Highlander party on old Maryville Pike, complete with nudes and mixed couples."

Bishop sent a copy of his letter to Walker.

A few days later, Walker wrote a four-page letter to the commission, explaining "his side" of the dispute. He did not deny having a role in the "dial-a-message" campaign. But he said "the Highlanders" seemed like a pretty suspicious bunch which holds "secret meetings" and "make out like they're teaching art, but nobody knows what kind of art."

Boycott Hinter

He said that he knew of attempts—which he indicated he felt were being pushed by Highlander—to organize a Negro "boycott" of Walker's grocery stores because of "high prices." But he indicated that the real reason for the boycott attempt was because of what he had been saying about Highlander.

The Highlander Research Center, Walker told the commission, was "run out of Monteagle," has brought "bad publicity" to Knoxville and has "caused the Police Department and the Sheriff's Office concern."

Walker said he had managed to infiltrate informers into a recent "secret meeting" at Highlander at which militant black power spokesman Stokely Carmichael was the main speaker.

Wants Probe

"If there's nothing wrong with this organization," Walker's letter said, "why don't they let the general public in on their workshops?" He said, "the things I have said about them are things that are public record and public knowledge."

Walker suggested that "someone in authority, such as the (House) Un-American Activities Committee" investigate Highlander. "At the same time, I would welcome them to investigate me and let's find out once and for all who is the red-blooded American..."

★ *Knoxville News-Sentinel,* January 17, 1967

"Lane Tries in Vain for Highlander Probe: Both Resolutions Tabled"

NASHVILLE, Jan. 17—Rep. Odell Cas Lane (R., Knoxville) introduced in the House today two resolutions calling for an investigation into the controversial Highlander Center in Knoxville—and both were promptly tabled....

One resolution called for the formation of a select committee of two Senators and three Representatives to investigate the activities of the centering organizations affiliated therewith." The other resolution called for an investigation by the attorney general, Highway Patrol, Tennessee Bureau of Criminal Identification, the Knoxville Police Department and the Knox County Sheriff's office "to cut this cancerous growth from our state and cast it out to die in the richness of Americanism and loyalty."

The erstwhile resolution said that the center, the successor of the old Highlander Folk School at Monteagle, has long been "haven for Communists, extreme leftists, fellow travelers and those who are in sympathy with those who advocate the violent overthrow of our Government." The resolution said the school is "nothing more than a front for wild parties, a headquarters for plots and dark schemes." It said that "a link to Highlander and its founder, (Myles) Horton," can be found in "nearly every riot in these United States in recent years."

"There have been lots of rumors, going around about this place," Lane told *The News-Sentinel* Nashville Bureau before the resolutions were tabled. "Some rumors that a lot of people don't know much about."

"And I think that if these rumors aren't true, then Highlander ought to be cleared."

He was asked if he was introducing the resolution at the insistence of his uncle, Knoxville Councilman Cas Walker.

"No, I haven't talked to him about this particular resolution, but I have talked to him about another Highlander resolution." . . .

Even so, Lane reflected his politician uncle's outspoken opposition to Highlander Center, his resolution saying "Highlander Center" for more than 30 years has been a cancerous growth. . . .

Editor's Note: Legislators from Knoxville supported the call for a state investigation, with the single exception of Robert Booker, who charged that the measure was an attempt "to satisfy the petty prejudices and political chicanery of local demagogues."

★ *Knoxville News-Sentinel*, April 12, 1967

"Highlander Probe Delayed in Senate"

... Rep. Robert Booker, who said he knows many of those connected with Highlander, declared the charges of "Communists and subversives" at the school "are untrue. I live five blocks from the school and some of these people are my friends."

Booker claimed that Lane had several reasons for asking for the investigation, including:

> 1. "In the early days, Highlander was really a labor school, teaching workers across the South how to organize. There still are some anti-labor people in my county."
> 2. "Persons sympathetic to Highlander planned a boycott against a local (Knoxville) supermarket chain which did not hire Negroes."

Lane, replying to Booker's charge concerning the supermarket chain, said the Cas Walker Store chain with which he is connected has "been working Negroes longer than any other grocery store in Knoxville."

★ Bob Booker

Well, of course I knew Myles Horton. From the day I got involved in the civil rights effort, I got to know Myles Horton. I knew what the Highlander Center stood for. It believed in rights of laboring people; it believed in rights of black people. So, they had people coming in for conferences and to talk about methods to get the job done.

Unfortunately, one time they had a known Communist who came, and that was a real bugaboo for us here in Knoxville to be associated with Communists—that's how Dr. Martin Luther King got smeared, for cohorting with Communists—because this man happened to visit the Highlander Center.

The vivid memories I have are that the police department was often sicced on the Highlander, because there was race mixing going on there. It had nothing to do with civil rights eating at lunch counters, but there possibly may have been blacks and whites mixing together socially and in the bedroom or whatever.

So, the police would raid at 3:00 or 4:00 in the morning, and the newspapers would report that they found people "partially clad."

I said, "Hell, if they raided my house at 3:00, they'd find me totally unclad!" Because I don't wear anything in the bed.

But it was this kind of foolishness. And then to top all of that off, there was a fire in Highlander on East Clinch when they were in that facility there. Assistant Fire Chief Bob Green made a statement to one of the newspapers: "You should've seen the Communist literature that we found when we went to put out the fire!"

So I was bold enough because I had gotten into government, I called Chief Green and said, "What kind of Communist literature did you find?"

"Well, I don't know, because I'm not an educated man, and I really don't deal in all that stuff."

I said, "Well, are you talking about the *Communist Manifesto*? Are you talking about Hitler's *Mein Kampf*?" And I named several. I said, "If you go to Lawson McGhee Library you'll find much more there than you found at Highlander Folk Center."

That kind of thing—I was constantly challenging people with this foolishness that they would come up with.

That truly was my connection with Highlander until I defended Highlander as a member of the legislature. When the city of Knoxville, including Cas Walker perhaps—I'm sure Mayor Lindon [Leonard Reid] Rogers and others—had the state representative Odell Cas Lane introduce a resolution against Highlander.

I said, "Now, wait a minute, Highlander is in my district!" In fact, just down the street from where I lived at the time.

So I made my first speech in the legislature opposing this resolution. Of course, the resolution was passed, but I got some accolades for standing up for Highlander and saying what I thought. In fact, I have the speech I made before the legislature!

So that was really my connection with Highlander. I never attended any meetings in Highlander. I admired Myles Horton and the people who worked there. But I was too busy working with my student body trying to get them together, to get the job done in desegregating theaters and lunch counters and dealing with the black community.

★ *Knoxville News-Sentinel,* October 15, 1967

"City Election Campaign is Nearing Peak: Most Interest Is Centered on Race for Mayor; Highlander Is Issue"

A statement made by Rev. Matthew A. Jones Sr., a Negro Episcopal priest who got into the mayor's race late, may indicate that the Negro population is more stirred up over the Highlander Center issue than some had expected. The statement was made Thursday when candidates appeared before the Triad Club, a Negro businessmen's group.

Candidates Garrison and Webster have called for a local investigation of Highlander.

At the Triad meeting Mr. Jones said he would consider any fight against the center "a fight against me."

"The drive for Civil Rights was started at Highlander," he said.

The Negro population makes up about 15 percent of Knoxville's population and could be a deciding factor in a close election.

Never Made Public

City Councilman Cas Walker, who is seeking re-election to a four-year term, constantly hammers at Highlander. He has said he has information about subversive activities at the center, but he has never made it public or turned it over to enforcement authorities.

The Legislature, under a resolution sponsored by Rep. Odell Lane, Mr. Walker's nephew, and Sen. Fred Berry, voted an investigation of Highlander this year, but none has been made. The American Civil Liberties Union has asked that the resolution be declared unconstitutional.

★ Randy Tyree

That was the time of the Red Scare and so anything unorthodox or out of the ordinary or anything that was occurring that somebody could latch onto that reinforced their own biases, and the Highlander Center was on the cutting edge, particularly in East Tennessee. The Highlander Center, my first memory of that was hearing about a cell—a Communist cell—right here in Knoxville. *Right in your backyard.*

I don't think it was personal with Cas. I think he was a quasi-racist in the sense that he would demagogue issues, perhaps, but in thinking back, not only the votes he got—he always ran strong in the black community—so it's an enigma wrapped in a confused state, I guess. That's what makes his history so almost revolutionary, in the timespan that he served and was alive and accomplished things.

Civil Rights and Sit-ins

★ Bob Booker

He was against progress, but I would never say he was racist in any way. I never detected that of Cas, never.

In the effort to desegregate Knoxville he was on our side. When we were demonstrating in downtown Knoxville to get the lunch counters desegregated, Cas Walker, John Duncan Sr., and former mayor George Dempster all said, "We need to do this thing on a peaceful basis. Let's get it done."

Cas never was negative about any of that. In fact, I'm always delighted to say that the leadership in the city of Knoxville was enlightened because they refused to let agitators get away with stuff, to beat up on people.

And Duncan made sure that policemen who had the right temperament were on Gay Street during that time. They arrested people who got out of line, but they weren't gonna use billy clubs on people, they didn't have police dogs, they weren't gonna call out the fire hoses, because the leadership in this town—John Duncan Sr., Cas Walker, and George Dempster—said, "We're not gonna have that here."

So, it was quite different in Knoxville from other places.

Zimbabwe Motavou

Editor's note: Zimbabwe Motavou was willing to talk about Cas, but he declined my request to record our conversation. What follows is my remembrance, based on handwritten notes, of an interview he granted me on Wednesday, July 12, 2017.

★ Joshua S. Hodge

In 1971, Zimbabwe Motavou helped lead a boycott against several grocery stores in Knoxville, including Cas Walker's stores, the White stores, IGA, and Kroger's.

Cas had always employed black people, but protesters complained that Cas limited black workers to menial jobs. They wanted to see African Americans work as managers, butchers, or cashiers. Cas's most profitable stores existed in black communities, at Five Points and on Western Avenue.

The protests took place originally around the perimeter of Cas's parking lot, not along the front of the store. Sherman Donaldson, a longtime Lonsdale resident, took the picket lines from the parking lot to the front of the store. In response, Cas would shut the stores down temporarily.

As the boycott continued, Cas met with Zimbabwe on three occasions to discuss the end of the organized and ongoing protest. Their conversations were "cordial" and "quite proper," in Zimbabwe's words. Cas was a "gentleman." Yet when Zimbabwe insisted that Cas change his hiring practices, the conversations fell apart. In the last of their meetings, Cas asked whether Zimbabwe and other protestors wished to combine their resources to buy his store. Zimbabwe said no.

Cas played hardball. He got an injunction against the protesters, stating that they needed to stay at least three hundred feet from the front door. He then sent infiltrators into the picket lines to start fights and generally disrupt the peaceful protests. Any sort of chaos in the protests favored Cas's position.

It just so happened that 1971 was the summer when Mary Tindell burst into Cas's "Farm and Home Hour" studio. Though reports differ, the altercation took place live on the air and ended abruptly with Cas dragging Tindell out the door by her hair. Cas's protestors, including Motavou, called on Cas to be removed from the city council for the incident but to no avail. They also decried his commercials that were insensitive to the black community—such as the commercial in which a young African American child eats watermelon and grins—even though Cas claimed never to have meant anything derogatory by it.

As I listened to Motavou recall these events, I wondered what he thought of Cas as a person and what Cas's relationship to Knoxville's black community was in the end. Zimbabwe recalled that Cas was "condescending, but that was the orthodoxy." Cas had been the face of Knoxville for decades, and that is why labor activists chose to boycott him in the early 1970s, according to Motavou.

I also told Motavou about Booker's description of city leaders as "enlightened."

"Bob isn't unique in that thinking," Motavou replied. It was hard to see the city leadership as such from Motavou's perspective. To make changes within the city, he said, "sit-in movements were required." If city leaders were so "enlightened," he argued, then why did sit-ins have to occur at all? Why did he and others have to protest at Rich's Department Store? Why did black kids have scuffles with the very white kids they had grown up with their entire lives?

When I asked Motavou about Cas Walker's legacy for the city of Knoxville, however, he proposed that Walker was only part of the problem. He put it this way: "There were folks who believed as Cas Walker believed, who either singularly or collectively had more power to keep Knoxville from progressing when it comes to race than Cas Walker."

★ Bradley Reeves

The "Thumpin' Good" commercial—that, I remember as a kid. Rows of little black children, heads down, completely horrible images . . . but with a catchy theme song, it was a reggae influence.

It doesn't exist—I thought [I] found the box for it, and I thought, "This is it, we've found it!" It's an old two-inch quad videotape. It was empty. There was a big marker on it that said "erase." I thought, "Somebody got smart."

If you talk to African-Americans of a certain age, they're pro-Cas, more so than a lot of the white folks of a certain age. . . .

I don't think he was a racist. I don't think he was. But he knew the advantage of hiring African Americans and opening up stores in the African American communities when no one else would. You could look down on that; there's always the activists that are just saying, "He just did it to make money off of them!"

But when you actually ask an African American—don't get me wrong, I'm the most liberal guy you'll ever meet, but I can see two sides of the story; I can be right smack dab in the middle—I'll talk to people over in the barbecue joints over on Magnolia. "Cas Walker—I love that guy! He'd send flowers to my mother's funeral. He gave us jobs."

In his stores, the whites and the blacks ate together. And that was before the 1964 Civil Rights Act. It just—I don't know. I don't think he was all bad; I don't think he was all good.

"One night's catch of racoons," with Cas Walker and Jerry Morrison.
Photo courtesy of Pat and Ken Paul. No date provided.

CHAPTER 9

"The Ole Coon Hunter"

In many of his promotions, Cas Walker liked to describe himself as the "ole coon hunter." As this chapter shows, friends and family accompanied Walker on hunting trips into northeastern Georgia. Some loved the experience while others dreaded it, but anyone who went experienced a wild ride. Over the years, Cas corresponded with *Full Cry* magazine, through which he bought and traded "coon dogs" with other avid hunters. Even in old age, Cas continued to espouse the moral and health benefits of raccoon hunting and even suggested that his long years of running dogs through the woods in search of varmints had given him beautiful legs.

Coon Hunting in Georgia

★ James Bragg

I went coon hunting with him one time, and that was the last time I ever want to do it. It sounded so great. But I was a little kid.

So we went coon hunting; actually, we were running the dogs. For him it wasn't killing the coons. I've got pictures, Cas with like twenty-five dead coons or whatever.

But in the later years, it was purely the dogs. This is Cas as a younger man. He would say, "That's Old Blue," or, "That's Hoot," or whatever his dogs' names were. I couldn't tell one dog from the other.

But we would go through some of the swampiest places. It was so snaky looking. And he would say, "There's a cottonmouth."

I'm saying, "Do we have to? Can we go home?"

I was probably less than ten years old. And wherever he stepped, I stepped. I figured if it was safe that time, it was gonna be safe a second time. I was scared to death. It was way into the morning hours. Then you had to gather the dogs up.

He asked me a hundred times. I never went back.

★ Larry Mathis

We used to hunt down in Georgia—this was back in the early '60s. Of course, there weren't any coons up here. There was a few, but you'd just go down to Georgia and catch as many as you want to. I don't know whether they even had a season down there on them or not. We'd hunt in the summertime, things like that.

We'd go, and it was in a swampy area. Cas would wear knee-boots, because sometimes you may be wading in water a foot deep or something like that.

He'd go back to his hotel room with that old black mud on his boots and just lay down on the bed. We got to where they weren't too many hotels in that little old town that would rent Cas a room.

Anyhow, I remember, one time, we were in a hotel room in Perry, Georgia. I never will forget this. Cas got up that morning, and at that time, he wore—you know what long johns are?—these were short-sleeve and short-legged long johns, but they were made in one piece, like you'd take a pair of shorts and a T-shirt together. Cas had that on. He got up—I never will forget—he got up and he scratched a little bit, then he walked over to the mirror. He got his toothbrush out, no toothpaste, no water, no nothing. He took it and put it in his mouth and he scrubs about two or three times, then took his toothbrush and he brushed his hair.

I got to laughing. He looked around and said, "Ha ha!, that's the advantage of being bald—you can brush your teeth and your hair with the same brush!"

★ Bruce Wheeler

I invited him to my history class a couple of times, and he would talk about how he won elections. Politics in Knoxville was openly dirty. Undergraduates were stunned by his stories about how he had gotten drunks to come out and pass out literature for his opponent and things like that.

I had him in class twice, but the problem was you could never keep him on the subject. He would just ramble. I don't think he was losing it; it was just the way he was.

Because he was talking about raccoon hunting, which the undergraduates couldn't have cared less about, and he said how good it was for your health, and he turned around and he pulled up his pants legs and he said, and I quote, "Many women have cried themselves to sleep at night because they don't have legs like this."

And they looked like little elephant stumps.

Dogs and Horses

★ Bob Lutrell

I'll tell you about that time he went hunting down there in Georgia, and somebody was trying to steal his dog. Well, he was down there hunting, and his dog didn't come in. It was his favorite dog, so he got in the car and thought, "Well, I'll just ease down the road here and maybe we'll see him jumping a fence or doing something and I'll get him."

So he saw this guy loading his dog up in his truck, and he hollered at him. The guy shut the door and took off. Before he got in the car, Cas pulled his shotgun out and shot him in the butt! The guy took off and went to the nearest town down the road and told the sheriff what had happened.

So Cas went on down the road and followed him. He went to this town and the police pulled him over. He said, "What's the matter?"

"You're supposed to go to jail with me. They've got a complaint down there."

He went down there and they said, "The guy filed a complaint for your arrest and says you shot him in the butt."

He says, "Well, it must have been that guy that was stealing my dog."

He told them about that. He got his dog back, but the guy filed a complaint on him: "Some guy shot me with a shotgun, buckshot!"

I don't think Cas meant to kill him, but he wanted him to know he had the wrong dog in the car!

★ Bennie Wallen Jean

I want to tell you about the coon hunters magazine, *Full Cry* magazine. It's published in Sedalia, Missouri. And he would write a letter probably every month, and he'd talk about his coon dogs. . . .

He would sell coon dogs by that, too. And I know there was a coon dog he wanted to sell. The dog's name was Redbone. So, one day he was gone out to lunch, and he got a call about that Redbone dog. By writing the ad

Cas with stuffed raccoon, December 17, 1981. Printed by permission of the *Knoxville News Sentinel*.

and all this, I felt like I was good friends to Redbone so I told him all about Redbone. I can't remember if he was silent on the trail or chopped at the track now, I don't remember now which one he was, but I told him all about the dog and everything. I told him how much the dog cost, so he said he was going to send a money order.

I think it was about $500. I'm pretty sure it was 500.

So anyway, I sold the dog, and Mr. Walker came in and I said, "I sold Redbone."

"You did?"

So I told him all the details, the man's address, phone number, I told him everything about it. And he said, "Well, I'm just gonna have to put you in charge of sellin' my dogs!"

We would ship dogs in a crate. He had somebody that he paid to make crates to put the dogs in and we shipped them by air. The funny thing about shipping the dogs . . . one day, it was absolutely pouring down rain, and I had been bugged all day; it was really hectic for me that day, and I was sittin' there thinking, "What else can go wrong?"

I get this phone call and it's this: "This is Delta Airlines at the Knoxville airport. Your dog has broken out of his crate, and he's runnin loose on the airport and we can't catch him. Can you come and catch that dog?"

I laughed and I said, "You know, I'm not into catching dogs." But I said. "I'll get a hold of Mr. Walker's handyman, and I'll send him out there to get the dog."

And he said, "I wish you'd hurry; I'm so afraid he's gonna get in the way of a plane taking off."

I called and I think I called every store, and I was about to think I wasn't gonna find him, so finally I got a hold of him, and he took another crate out there and they caught the dog and shipped it.

You see, my life was so interesting!

★ Rowdy Cope

Mr. Walker, if he was out somewhere, he didn't go hide in the corner to keep from talking to people. In fact, he'd tell it like it is. If he thought it, he said it!

I think he made a lot friends that way. They didn't think he was an uppity millionaire that didn't want to talk to nobody.

He was a millionaire and you know what he drove for about twenty-five to thirty years? A '56 Nash Rambler with a dog box in the back of it!

That's the car I learned to drive on. I was twelve years old, eleven or twelve years old, and we had just had a pony sale over in Chilhowie Park.

[*Cas imitation*] "Preacher [*a nickname of Rowdy's*], get in my car and go to Holloway Farmers and get some buckets."

But the biggest thing he ever got me on: we were in Newport at a horse show, back at the old fairgrounds, before there was an interstate. We were up there, had a nine-horse van, with eight or nine horses in it, and showing.

And the horse trainer got drunk. The truck driver got drunk.

Cas turned around and said, "Preacher, load them horses and take them home." I was lucky, that drunk wasn't so far gone that he couldn't tell me to go through five and hit the button, go through five more. I was driving an International with a Road Ranger transmission in it. Pulled a nine-horse trailer, eighteen-wheeler down the old road back to Knoxville to Third Creek Lane.

I was fourteen years old. Mr. Walker seemed to think I could do about anything, and that's why I worked for him that long.

★ *Knoxville News-Sentinel,* March 19, 1976

"Cas Gives Lesson on Habits, Morals of Coons and Hunters" by Jim Balloch

NASHVILLE—Knoxville grocer Cas Walker extolled the virtues of coons and coon-hunting to the Senate yesterday and asked the lawmakers not to pass a bill that would outlaw training of coon dogs out of season. Walker was the guest of Sen. Fred Berry, Senate sponsor of the bill, which was drawn up by the State Wildlife Resources Agency.

With his hat tilted back on his head and occasionally grasping his suspenders, Walker said the practice of training dogs by letting them chase coons out of season is not the main cause of diminishing coon populations in some areas. "A lot of you might not know this, but Mr. Coon only has one girl friend, and he runs with her all the time and no more, and that's why we don't have any more coons. Their morals are better than ours, sometimes," he said.

Walker, who says he has been hunting coons for 62 years, admitted, "We may have a few scalawags who might kill a coon out of season, but that's rare."

He described coon hunters as spirited folks "who like to hear them dogs . . . a coon hunter has no interest in a deer. You could run a deer right by me and I wouldn't shoot it, but I'll lay all night trying to outsmart Mr. Coon."

Coon hunters are also men of integrity, he added. "A natural born coon hunter is not a liquorhead or a petticoat chaser," Walker said. . . .

The Senate adopted a resolution honoring Walker for his many political and public accomplishments and for his expertise as a coon hunter and coon dog trainer.

"I Got Trouble"

★ Bo Pierce

But I remember here's this picture of him, sitting at one of his checkout lanes, I think it was the Walker Boulevard store out toward Fountain City. He had been on his TV show. Of course, he had had farms in outlying areas, and a lot of barns, and he had a rat problem at one of them. And he'd got on TV and telling his worshippers out there that would do anything for Cas, he said, "I need some ratters, I need some good cats that are good ratters that I can take to my barns that'll get rid of my rats." He said, "Just bring them out to Walker Blvd. store."

I mean, they flooded the store with cats! Somebody calls the health department and they come in on him. Somebody took a picture of him at a counter, and it was just this kind of resigned look on his face, like, "I got trouble."

★ *Knoxville News-Sentinel*, March 23, 1983

"Cas Walker Says . . ."

UNUSUAL ANNOUNCEMENT:

Wanted 500 housecats delivered to the Cas Walker Kennel on Third Creek Road. That is just off Middlebrook Pike, or right across the street from the Gulf Oil Company. Claude Maxwell is the manager. These cats will be fed, taken care of, and they will be trained for ratters.

Remember we want 500 cats, and we wouldn't care if we had them all within 30 days. Then from here on out you can bring all the cats you have and they will all go to different farms and be turned loose. It's foolish to take an animal's life, for no reason at all.

We might even give away a big, pretty cat with a dozen regular size cans of cat food. Who knows, I have sold pigs out of grocery store windows at $10 each, with 100 pounds of hog feed. The ole timers will remember this, when I had a store at 35 Market Square. There were more unusual things happening then, than there is now. Of course, the World's Fair might brighten this up.

★ *Knoxville News-Sentinel*, May 20, 1983

"Health Officers Tell Cas No Cat-Collecting" by Bill Maples

The furor over Cas Walker and his determination to collect cats for distribution among East Tennessee dairy farms may have reached a Mexican standoff between Walker and the Knox County Health department.

The health department says Walker cannot keep cats in his Walker Boulevard grocery store, where food for human consumption is sold. The health department made that clear to Walker yesterday.

Walker says his lawyer has told him he can collect cats at the store, and he is going to keep on collecting them.

Members of the Knox County Humane Society saw that 14 of the cats were removed from outside the Walker Boulevard store yesterday. And Walker said today he will seek a court order to get the cats back, if it is necessary to ensure they will not be destroyed.

"They were taken illegally," he said. "If I can be assured that won't be killed I won't ask for the court order."

Linda Ford, member of the societies board, said she, other Society members and people who like cats found the cats crowded and the cages in the produce room of the store. She said they notified the health department, which sent a representative to tell the store manager he could not keep cats in the store.

Miss Ford said Society members asked the manager what he wanted to do with the cats, and he said he did not care. She said the animal control office of the city sent officers, who picked up the cats and took them to the Animal Shelter.

Miss Ford said the cats were crowded into the cages and seemed upset by the surroundings and little food was available for them. She said the members visited Walker's kennels on Third Creek Lane and found cats there which had wounds on their faces.

Walker denied yesterday the cats are being mistreated.

Yesterday afternoon, after the visit by humane officers in the representative of the health departments city food program, the hampers holding the cats have been moved outside the back door of the grocery store, and Walker was not insistent about moving them back inside, although he told his employees there:

"You work for me. You don't work for no health department, and you do as I say."

Walker flatly denied he was collecting the cats to sell to research laboratories. He also flatly denied he was collecting them to train his coon dogs. But he declined to name any dairy farm owner who had taken some of the cats.

"I don't want to embarrass anybody by saying he took some cats for me," He said. "But I can tell you this: a prominent lawyer in town just took 25 of them to put on his farm."

Walker, of course, says dairy farmers in particular need to catch mice and rats, which eat stored grain.

He was told this by a reporter: "What is causing all the furor is that people don't believe any farmer needs that many cats on his farm."

And Walker replied: "We only allow people to take 25 at a time."

Walker said environmentalists from the health department came to his office at Tennessee Valley advertising agency on Chapman Highway and threatened to have him arrested. Walker said he called police and an officer came to his office and then tried to arrest him without a warrant. He said he told the officer to go back and get a warrant and Walker would go to jail with him.

A spokesman for the health department said there was never any threat of arrest. He said health department personnel merely told Walker he could not keep cats in the Walker Boulevard store.

An official in the UT veterinary college says cats are not being used much for research. A Professor of environmental practice in the college says sellers of live cats for research have to have licenses from the U.S. Department of Agriculture. Buyers have to buy the cats from licensed dealers or have donation forms signed by the person providing the animals. Sellers must produce records on all cats they sell.

Walker solicited the animals in an ad in newspapers Monday.

The ad asked for 500 cats and said they would be put in kennels holding 20 each and taken to dairy farms where they would be cared for. Rat problems are common on dairy farms, and the cats would be used to rid the farms of them, Walker said.

"We are concerned about the health of these animals," Miss Ford said. "Is he inspecting them to see that they are healthy? Is he doing rabies inoculations? Or is he just going to drop them in the County?"

Miss Ford said if the animals are not neutered or spayed, 500 cats could very easily become 1000 or 5000 by September.

Walker said, "If they are so concerned about the cats' health, why are they killing them? It's a mockery with the animal shelter." An estimated 115 cats were destroyed at the shelter in April, members said.

Walker said he is giving the cats distemper, rabies and parvo shots. The cats will get all the shots they need before they're taken out to the farms, he said.

"But we sure don't spay or neuter them. We'd like to have more cats. We feed them every other day so they'll learn to hunt," he said.

Miss Ford said the Humane Society has received unsubstantiated reports in the past the cats were being used to train coon dogs, and she believes that is why the shelter stopped giving Walker cats.

Walker says he buys his coon dogs already trained, and he wouldn't have a dog that chases cats.

Walker said he would rather buy all of the cats in the county than see one of them destroyed by the shelter.

Mrs. Vicky McClellan, Director of the animal shelter on Millwood Road, said euthanasia, or putting the animals to sleep is preferable to letting them run wild in Knoxville.

Cas and the final edition of the *Watchdog,* December 16, 1981. Printed by permission of the *Knoxville News Sentinel.*

CHAPTER 10

The *Watchdog*
"The Unvarnished Naked Truth That Can Be Backed Up in Court"

From 1974 to 1981, Cas Walker published the *Watchdog*. In this weekly newspaper, Walker lambasted his political opponents and advised his customers on all manner of local, county, and state politics. According to some, locals formed long lines in front of Cas's stores to get the most recently published edition of his newspaper. Unfortunately for Cas, some of the paper's "Naked Truth" turned out instead to be libelous. In 1981, after a third libel case, a judge awarded a police officer the total worth of the newspaper, which effectively shut down its publication. With the *Watchdog* in tatters and Cas's television program ending in the early 1980s, his public voice lost much of its volume.

"It Was Pretty Well Informed"

★ Jack Sharp

His *Watchdog* newspaper came out once a week through his stores. And people—when you went by there to get it, you'd better, if you want to know what's going on. They'd be lined up waiting on them.

The *Journal* and *Sentinel* didn't like it, but it was pretty well informed. Because people would go to him or his people, and if you were interested—and most people were—they'd line up at night, waiting on those papers to get here. And I was one of them.

★ Carl Warner

The *Watchdog* worked this way: he had a company make him a special tape recorder. It was the only one that ever existed. Because normally a tape recorder reel was maybe three or five or seven inches. This one was three feet. Huge.

He would call from his home and dictate, and the tape recorder would record everything he said at his office. The tape recorder was not at his home but at the office. I'd come in the morning, and I'd transcribe from the tape recorder what he dictated for an article in the *Watchdog*. But it was never in order—he would say something, and after dinner he'd go back and say some more, but what he says now should be first, not second, after he said it.

Then, the next morning, he would wake up and he would dictate more. And my job was simply to put it all together in order so that it made sense.

It was mostly, I'd say at least 90 percent of the *Watchdog* was politics. He hated some of the members of the city council. He was a former mayor of Knoxville, and if he didn't like you, he just tore you apart in his columns.

There was a female member of the city council who he disliked—he just hated her guts! And I really had to kinda change some of the stuff up to keep him from being sued for libel. And I did that pretty well. We were threatened to be sued—I don't know—a half dozen times, but they never followed through while I was editor. Never got sued. The attorneys would say, "You don't stand a chance. Cas Walker would beat you. You're spending money for a lawsuit, but you won't get anywhere."

In some cases, the judge would even throw it out before it got to the court. They'd say, "This is a suit that makes no sense, and it has no legal bearing," and he just threw it out.

Basically, because I changed some of the things he says so that—I took courses in college when I was studying journalism, that had to do with law and the press, so I was very familiar with that.

But he used his paper for his own benefit, to get back at people he didn't like, for whatever reason.

The *Watchdog* was widely read, by all the members of the county court, the county commission, the city commission, the mayor, anyone that was connected with politics in any way, through job or running for office. That was widely read by those people. If you walked into the *Knoxville News-Sentinel*, you'd see the *Watchdog* on the desk of one of the reporters.

★ Bill Routh

My personal recollections of Cas Walker related to my father's business relationship with him. John C. (Casey) Routh was a retail advertising salesman with the *Knoxville News-Sentinel*. Cas, upon learning that my father had been promoted to display advertising, asked if Dad could work his account. This was due to Cas knowing my grandfather, William Ivory, who was a butcher for several businesses, and worked for Cas during the Great Depression.

Despite stories claiming Cas was difficult or hard to work with, Dad never had any problems with him. Cas was always accommodating and mindful of the newspaper's publishing schedule. At the time, the *News-Sentinel* was releasing several issues a day, beginning with an issue shipped to the Tri-Cities early in the morning. Cas was at the newspaper drafting an editorial that needed to run in the afternoon paper. Obviously, he knew the publishing deadlines.

Dad was taking dictation from Cas and writing the editorial, "Cas Walker says . . ." on a notepad. One of the other salesmen, possibly Fred Ramsey, looked over Dad's shoulder and said, "Casey, there's a mistake in the text."

Cas Walker looked at him, and replied, "Cas Walker's editorial is supposed to have mistakes."

★ Cas Walker, *My Life History*

When Elvis Died

I want to tell you how a picture of Elvis appeared on my "Watch Dog" paper.

I had a girl that worked for the "Watch Dog" and she was about the smartest thing I've ever seen. If I wanted to get something done, I'd tell her and she always come up with it.

I had one of those speakers in my car and Cal Madrick came through and said that Elvis Pressley [sic] had just died in Memphis. I got on my microphone and I asked my employee if she was in her car and she said she sure was. I said, "I've got something that I want to talk to you about. Let's just both go to my office, I just come up with this idea." She said that she would be there. We both got over and shut the door she said, "Was it something about Elvis Pressley?" I said, "Yes, I want you to go to Memphis tonight and stay at the hotel that I always stay. I want you to be at the courthouse in the morning at eight o'clock. The people that work there will be just getting there, but I want you to go talk with the first man you see, and tell him that you are representing the "Watch Dog" paper from Knoxville (one of the best known papers in East Tennessee) and they want a copy of Elvis Pressley's will."

They said, "I don't know wheather [*sic*] we can do that or not, but that paper seems to know about what they are doing. They say that a will is something that is public when a man dies. If something is public than [*sic*] anybody can get it." They said something about some other magazine they had been told would be there. She said, "Lord have mercy, they ain't no paper like the "Watch Dog" seems to be. I knew the mayor real well. They said, "I guess we'll just have to let you go ahead and read it."

She went ahead and got five or ten copies of it. I had told her, "You go on down from there over to the funeral home. They'll just be about ready to take Elvis down to Graceland. I want you to tell them that you are his niece, and you just go in, and you want to ride over to Graceland in the limousine with the body." They let her ride over, they let her open the casket, and they let her set it like she wanted it set for people to look at.

She took the cover off of his face and took a picture of him right in the casket. She took his photograph, and you know, we had his picture on the front page of the "Watch Dog" that week.

We had 10,000 wills made and we sold them for $1.00 apiece with every $10.00 grocery order. We sold every one of them. We had to print 10,000 for our out of town stores and we put them out and sold all of them that week.

We went back and had more printed to take down to Georgia and South Carolina and sold them to a gentleman at $1.50 each. We sold them for $2.00 with a twenty dollar order and they did well.

Winn Dixie had just gone in there, and we sold everything the same way and they took them. They went over real big and was one of the biggest deals we ever have done. I guess that was one of my greatest promotional ideas. It was good thinking on my part to send her down there to get that will.

★ Bob Booker

He published the *Watchdog* to pump up business—everybody had to get the *Watchdog*. They printed all—everything that was fit to print.

It had all kinds of stuff in it, including there were a couple of things about me in there. I'm happy to say, even though we started out as bitter enemies, there's this *Watchdog* of October 7, 1971. I was running for mayor of Knoxville. "Black mayor candidate Bob Booker has strong support"—and he talked about that in the article.

And then here's another, March 21, 1974, because I was standing up for things—well, I didn't like how the policemen were treating people in the black community, and I challenged them many times. So in this issue of the *Watchdog* Cas has the headline: "Police department trying to give Bob Booker a hard time." We got to be allies, even though we started out as bitter enemies.

So people would read the *Watchdog* and see what Cas had to say. I guess much of the stuff we took with a grain of salt, but sometimes I wrote for the *Watchdog* in Cas's style. The articles weren't attributed to me, but I could say "them that's" and whatever, and I would write that stuff in the *Watchdog*.

★ Ben Walker

Yeah, Cas used to get on TV and talk about people. He didn't care, it didn't matter if it was the president of the United States. But most of it was politicians of Knox County. He'd get on there, and my daddy would shake his head sometimes and say, "Somebody's gonna kill him."

The *Watchdog*—politicians did not like the *Watchdog*! I remember he used to publish people maybe out here in North Knoxville that were payin' $300 for property tax. And then he'd have a big home in West Knoxville, and he'd say, "These people are payin' the same amount!"

I don't know if that's true or not, but I remember seein' the pictures in the *Watchdog*. And the only reason the politicians were angry is because they didn't get to do some shenanigans that they wanted to do. That's the reason they didn't like Cas.

★ The *Watchdog*, September 15, 1977

"THE WARNER REPORT—The Truth Is Coming!" by Carl Warner

In almost 20 years of newspaper and radio-television reporting I have never permitted anyone as a result of a payoff promise or by an implied or direct threat to influence what I report. I shall continue to report the truth, regardless of recent bribe attempts and threats!

One of the reasons that my personal admiration and respect for Cas Walker has continued to grow is that Mr. Walker has never attempted in any way to influence what I report in the *Watchdog*.

I have only received two instructions from Mr. Walker regarding my *Watchdog* position: 1. To be sure of the facts in order that the *Watchdog* would not be on the losing end of a possible libel suit: and second, to help the *Watchdog* be a force in the community that would cause politicians and others to think twice before committing acts of dishonesty or a breach of the public trust. In the event of a specially controversial subject, Mr. Walker asks simply, "Do we have the facts," and "Is it the truth?"

In this modern 20th century world it is sad but true that Cas Walker is a vanishing breed. He is one of the last remaining newspaper publishers who have the guts, courage and dedicated responsibility to print the truth. It is of course unfortunate that Knoxville's two daily newspapers and three television stations for years have grossly short-changed the citizens of this community. It appears therefore that the *Watchdog* published by Cas Walker is the only real newspaper in this town.

Cas Walker has been hoping that the other Knoxville media will eventually tell the truth about certain city and county public officials and a certain possible gubernatorial candidate and reveal the real story behind several highly controversial local and state issues. So far they haven't.

Now it's up to the *Watchdog*!

"Cas's Truth"

★ Julia Tucker

His paper came out sometimes twice a week but always once a week. And people just waited for it, because it was the *Watchdog*! It told things that nobody else knew. Some of them were true, some of them were false.

He was a bigoted man. OK, he was very class conscious, but I think one of the driving things that he had was that he was gonna become more than he was. And I admire that in him. He was more than the coal miner and the guy from up in the hills. And he could do this: he knew human nature, he knew what it took to get ignorant people to follow him, and also other people that were in fear of him. He commanded respect.

And he also had the press, he had ink. And I'm telling you, having that newspaper gave him power. And you don't ever argue with people that have ink. They win. That paper was a powerhouse in its day. I'm so glad somebody's kept them all.

I would say that his door at the paper was ever open to anybody that wanted to come in and tell a truth or a nontruth. And if it appealed to him, he would follow it, like an ant trail.

He was smart as a whip. He would take a grain of truth and turn it into an absurdity that people would believe.

People want to believe that somebody's out there fighting for them. That they're the underdog, and somebody's gonna tell them the truth. They got Cas's truth.

★ Bob Booker

There was a statement at the head of the *Watchdog* that really would get me. "The *Watchdog* publishes the unvarnished naked truth that can be backed up in court"—but that's not true, because he slandered a city policeman. A city policeman took him to court and won the worth of the *Watchdog*. Whatever Cas had in the *Watchdog* the court awarded the policeman, and the *Watchdog* went out of business.

★ *Knoxville News-Sentinel*, c. July 31, 1981

"Didn't Go Out of Town to Dodge Testifying,
Mrs. Tucker Tells Court" by Roger Harris

City School Board Chairman Julia Tucker yesterday denied that she purposely left town to avoid testifying in the libel trial against millionaire grocer Cas Walker.

Mrs. Tucker also denied that her testimony against Walker was an attempt by her to get even with Walker for bringing her name up in the trial.

Mrs. Tucker testified in Knox County Circuit Court yesterday in former city school board member Jack Cooper's $13 million libel suit against Walker. Cooper has accused Walker of defaming him, his wife and daughter in a series of stories that ran in the *Watchdog*, Walker's throwaway newspaper.

Judge T. Edward Cole yesterday recessed the trial until Aug. 10 to allow three jurors to take family vacations that had been planned prior to the trial.

Walker has repeatedly accused Mrs. Tucker of writing or furnishing the information for the stories about Cooper. Mrs. Tucker denied that she had anything to do with the stories.

Likewise, Walker has denied that he had anything to do with the stories other than changing a few words. Walker claims that he didn't even see most of the stories until they appeared in the *Watchdog*.

Mrs. Tucker was subpoenaed by Judge Cole since neither Cooper's or Walker's attorney was going to call her as a witness. Heated exchanges between Mrs. Tucker and Walker's attorney, W. P. Boone Dougherty, highlighted the school board chairman's testimony. Dougherty questioned the timing of Mrs. Tucker's trips out of town which coincided with this week's trial and the original trial date last September.

"You have been avoiding in every way you could to avoid appearing in this matter, haven't you?" Dougherty asked.

Mrs. Tucker responded by saying that her trips were business-related and the timing was one of those things beyond people's control—"like getting sick."

Dougherty asked her if this was a reference to getting sick last September, which forced a postponement of the trial. Mrs. Tucker said she was speaking generally and not referring to Dougherty's illness.

Dougherty also asked Mrs. Tucker if in fact she wasn't really out of state, but "up on a lake 20 miles from here." She said her trip this week was out of state. She did not say where. One report had her being in Colorado.

Dougherty also asked Mrs. Tucker if it wasn't true that she and Art Miller, former Knoxville television newsman, had written the stories about Cooper.

"That's a lie," Mrs. Tucker said.

Dougherty then asked Mrs. Tucker if she and Miller hadn't visited the Ramada Inn in West Knoxville together. Mrs. Tucker, obviously upset with the question, replied forcefully, "No, we did not."

Dougherty accused Mrs. Tucker of trying to get even with Walker. "Isn't it a fact that you said if he (Walker) brought your name up in this trial you would get even with him?"

"No," Mrs. Tucker said. "How in the world would I get even with Mr. Walker. I'd have to buy me a newspaper."

Dougherty also asked Mrs. Tucker if it was true she was the source for the stories in the *Watchdog* that said beer trucks owned by liquor dealer Mose Lobetti were used to distribute campaign literature in Holston Hills for Mrs. Tucker's 1977 campaign opponent, Phyllis Severance. Mrs. Tucker said she was not the source and added she had never seen beer trucks in Holston Hills where she lived.

In an attempt to discredit her testimony, Dougherty accused Mrs. Tucker of violating the Sunshine Law by frequently meeting with other school board members without public disclosure to discuss school issues. Mrs. Tucker said that wasn't true. Dougherty characterized Mrs. Tucker as a "hard-nosed politician" who campaigned vigorously. Mrs. Tucker said she considers herself a "servant of the people" and not a politician.

At one point during Dougherty's sometimes intense examination of Mrs. Tucker, Judge Cole suggested that Dougherty act like "the gentleman I know you are."

When questioned by Cooper's attorney, Keith McCord, Mrs. Tucker said she was asked by Cooper to try to get Walker to stop printing stories about Cooper. She said Walker told her, "I'm not through with the little bastard yet."

Walker, who testified yesterday after Mrs. Tucker, said he didn't make that statement about Cooper. "I ain't called anyone a bastard—yet," Walker said. Walker repeated the assertion he had made numerous times in the first three days of the trial that Mrs. Tucker was the writer or source for the stories about Cooper and that he did not doubt their accuracy because he trusted Mrs. Tucker.

The 78-year-old-grocer accused Mrs. Tucker of taking "slander language" that he is well-known for and using it in the stories about Cooper so that readers of the *Watchdog* would think that he wrote the stories. Walker characterized this slang usage as one of Mrs. Tucker's campaign tactics. "Don't be fooled by that lily white. . . . She's rough. I mean plenty rough. When they get too tough for me they're getting vicious," Walker said.

Walker also said that he would have printed a correction or an apology if Cooper had told him that the stories were inaccurate.

Mrs. Tucker also testified that prior to her first campaign for the school board in 1973 Walker advised her she needed to get something derogatory about Cooper to use against him. Mrs. Tucker said she told Walker she didn't think that was possible. Walker then told her, Mrs. Tucker said, if something couldn't be found, "I'll make it up."

Mrs. Tucker said she had no reason to write derogatory stories about Cooper because she respected him and had worked with him on PTA committees at Holston High School where their children attended school there. She said her relationship with Cooper was so friendly that when she decided to oppose him for the school board she went to Schubert Lumber Co. where Cooper works and told him of her intentions.

Mrs. Tucker said she did provide information to Walker for stories that appeared in the *Watchdog* on metro government and school closings but that what she wrote "wasn't recognizable" when it appeared in the *Watchdog*. She said she only provided the information at Walker's request.

Walker, however, said Mrs. Tucker was always writing stories praising herself or running down Cooper and "might-near lived" at the Tennessee Valley Advertising Agency.... Walker is president of the agency....

★ *Knoxville News-Sentinel,* December 16, 1981

"Walker Is Folding Watchdog" by Jacquelyn B. McClary

When the *Watchdog*, Cas Walker's throwaway publication, appears tomorrow, get hold of one and don't throw it away—it may become a collector's item.

Yesterday, following a meeting of the Knox County Housing Authority, Walker said he is shutting down the publication of the *Watchdog*, and this week's issue will be the last of the 17-year-old weekly. Walker considered the possibility of discontinuing the paper earlier, but he had not said anything specific.

Walker, a millionaire, recently testified that he started the *Watchdog* to promote his chain of grocery stores in Tennessee, Kentucky, and Virginia and to provide a forum for his political views. He said he started the paper to air his political views since the two daily newspapers would not give him fair coverage.

"It has gotten to be too much," he said. "This last judgment will open up the door to that many more suits."

Last week Walker lost a libel suit brought by Police Officer Wade E. Dunaway, who had been accused of "getting away with murder" in a series of Watchdog stories that began shortly after the shooting death of Robert Webb, Oct. 15, 1977. Dunaway was exonerated by a Knox County Grand Jury.

Attorney W.P. Boone Dougherty and Cas Walker, c. 1981.
Printed by permission of the *Knoxville News Sentinel*.

The suit cost Walker $182,765, the estimated value of Walker's Tennessee Valley Advertising Agency, publisher of the *Watchdog*. But it was not the first time stories printed in the *Watchdog* resulted in a suit. Many suits have been filed over the years for what has been called "libelous, irresponsible reporting." A number of suits involved pictures of persons reported by the *Watchdog* as having written bad checks to Cas Walker–operated grocery stores.

Walker said he never had a judgment against him before. He settled a suit back in August brought by former city school board member Jack Cooper for an estimated $100,000 in the sixth day of the trial.

A suit is pending in Federal Court here against Walker brought by Henry Ellenburg, former executive director of the Knox County Housing Authority. Ellenburg also charged that the *Watchdog* published "false, malicious and defamatory statements" that he was unsuited for his position and would have to be fired. That case will be heard next month.

★ *Knoxville News-Sentinel,* December 17, 1981

"Cas Walker Looks Back as a Milestone is Reached" by Bill Maples

The long jaw set at a jaunty angle there for a moment, and the gravelly voice spoke confidently of the future. "I'm going to stay right here in Knoxville sellin' groceries. I ain't goin' to travel. Had enough of that. Been to Spain, Mexico, the Bahamas." It was Cas Walker, who passed a milestone yesterday when we saw his giveaway weekly publication, the *Watchdog,* arrive from the printer for distribution as the last issue. He had published the weekly for 17 years.

Walker, 78, who insists he should be called Cas, was sitting in the living room of his comfortable, though unpretentious, home at 2838 Gaston Ave. He was in his stocking feet after a long day of meetings with officials in his chain of grocery stores. The voice lowered and mellowed: "I'm older. Back when I was younger, my wife would fix my breakfast at 4 in the mornin' and I'd open up the grocery store at 5."

"I'm getting it in my mind to cut my coon huntin' 'way down. I got seven good coon hounds left. I'd quit when all of them have died or got killed huntin.'"

His 16 grocery markets and eight family stores in Tennessee, Kentucky, and Southwest Virginia, his love for the wild coon hunt at night, and his life in Knoxville took up much of the conversation.

He was born in the Sinks of Sevier County, near English Mountain and "Dr. DeLozier delivered me and they paid him one sheep." He grew up in the Fair Garden community, where his grandpa had a grocery. He worked seven years in the mines of Harlan County, Ky., and worked in the commissary when there was a strike. That was his first taste of grocering.

"The first day I took in $6.60. The first Saturday I took in $27.70. I figured I better drum up some trade. I had a few chicken in a coop—everybody bought their chickens live then. I advertised in the papers I was going to throw two dozen dominecker hens off the roof [of] the store the next Saturday, and anyone who caught them could have 'em. The women made aprons to catch them hens. The aprons cost more than the hens cost."

This drew large crowds, and they blocked the streets. "I'd get in jail for blocking the streets. It cost $10 to make bond. I hired an old man to go over and stay at the City Jail and make bond for me. Some Saturdays they'd haul me over there seven or eight times."

He opened his second store at Sneed and Willow Avenues five years later. The Cas Walker acumen for drawing crowds and making money was beginning to show.

"For Saturdays, I roasted peanuts and popped popcorn and made them real salty and sold them fer next to nuthin'. I found a whole truckload of soda pop over in Middlesboro for two cents a bottle. I put all this pop in tubs and iced it down, and mixed a few Cokes with it. After they'd been eating peanuts and popcorn a spell they'd say, 'Ain't you got somethin' cold to drink?' and I'd say, 'Sure buddy.' In the mines everybody was a buddy.

"I'd dig down in the ice and pull up one of them bottles. He'd say he wanted a Coke. I'd say, 'Why son, this here is a strawberry fizz. You ain't drunk nothin' 'till you've drunk a strawberry fizz.' I made $300 that day with the peanuts and popcorn and that truckload of pop."

The main reason for the folding of the *Watchdog* and Walker's apparent feeling he is at a turning point was his loss of a libel suit last week and the judgment against his Tennessee Valley Advertising Agency, publisher of the *Watchdog*, of $182,765.

He was asked several questions regarding the judgment. How much will this hurt? What is his net worth? Will he have to sell something if his appeal of the case fails?

"I have put a lot of money in real estate in the past few years," he said. "I don't have much wealth in cash, but I have several million in real estate. The judgment? I may have to sell the advertising agency."

He settled another libel suit earlier this year for what was reported to be $100,000. He has another suit pending in Federal Court here which concerns a *Watchdog* story.

He has said he is out of politics. Last night in his living room he qualified that. "If I'd thought I'd have to deal with politics as much as I have I'd a stayed on Council." (He served on the Knoxville City Council nearly 30 years, beginning in 1941, retiring in 1972, and was mayor for a time.)

"From here on out the only kind of politicians I'm goin' to have anything to do with is someone who won't embarrass me. The kind of politics I did was honest. I never did buy votes, but I'd feed a lot with chitlin' trots and such.

"I was in politics for years and nobody ever embarrassed me. But politics got bad in Knoxville 14 years ago. Now you look at it. The City's debt . . .

"I always talked the language of the common man and never tried to be anything but Cas Walker." This has been his stock in trade. His language in most cases is not that of an astute businessman who can look at a column of figures on a legal pad and reach the bottom line in a second or two.

He has been coon hunting since he was 8, and he bought his first pair of shoes with pelts he brought in from the night hunts. In his office at Tennessee Valley Advertising there is a painted display board six by eight feet called "Cas Walker's Coon Dog Cemetery." There are four dozen tombstones painted on the board, with the name of a favorite hound Cas once owned, and which was killed in the hunt or by other circumstances. There are tombstones reserved for the remaining hounds. "I drove 1500 miles to buy a silent trainer (a hound that doesn't bay until he has a coon treed)," he said. "Then I had to stand there in McIntosh, Fla., and watch an old coon drown 'im. The dog's name was Pap. The coon just grabbed 'im by the neck and pulled him down and held him on the bottom 'til he drowned. I went back down there later to hunt for that coon and seen 'im in a citrus orchard. I shot 'im in a tree. He must have been 14 years old."

His dogs have won national awards in Pennsylvania, Delaware, Maryland, and New Jersey and twenty-first place in international competition in Oblong, Ill.

Cas and his wife, the former Virginia Grantham, have lived in the neat cottage on Gaston Avenue 33 years. It is where they reared their only child, the late Wilma Matorin, and where three grandsons run in and out. Some years ago he built a masterpiece of a ranch home in the rolling hills east of Knoxville. Why didn't he ever move?

"I'm 78, and I get tired of a mornin'," he said. "I can run by here and lay down a while. Besides, my wife likes it here, and I got the best view in Knoxville." On a clear day you can see Mt. LeConte and all the beauty of the Smokies from Mrs. Walker's kitchen window.

What would he tell a young man starting in business now?

"It's hard to say," he said. "Business is harder, and I'm older, too."

Fire at Cas's grocery store in Pennington Gap, Virginia, 1961.
Printed by permission of the *Knoxville News Sentinel*.

CHAPTER 11

Troubles

Cas Walker sidestepped several adverse situations during his professional career, but he began to encounter significant troubles in the 1980s. In addition to the folding of the *Watchdog*, national morning shows replaced Walker's "Farm and Home Hour." Thereafter, Cas spent a few years in a nursing home for treatment of a medical condition. In the meantime, Virginia Walker died and left Cas to face the world without her. Since she had been by his side for the majority of his life, the decade appeared bleak to the "ole coon hunter." But Cas had dealt with problems before, and he would reemerge from the 1980s mostly unscathed. This chapter examines the not-so-pleasant moments of Walker's later life.

Tax Evasion and Ray Jenkins

★ Victor Ashe

Well, first of all, Cas didn't grow up with the same educational sophistication—although he had a lot of street smarts—and over the years, he made money. That's when he got indicted for income tax evasion, which he was acquitted on. And his famous line was: "I paid my taxes, I've sent out more than one of those missiles."

Ray Jenkins defended him, and Ray was the perfect lawyer for him, a noted, successful lawyer for people who got in trouble. He got an East Tennessee jury. They were no more gonna convict Cas of tax evasion than . . . they just weren't gonna do it.

And the Feds made the mistake of sending down some prosecutor from D.C., who looked like he was a prosecutor from D.C. He walked in the room and lost before he started.

Ray was a very colorful lawyer. He obviously had a law degree because he practiced law and he was educated, but he also had a country air about him that he portrayed particularly before the jury very well.

He'd say of the other lawyers, "We're glad to have these gentlemen from the District of Columbia down here. Now, be nice to them!" He never attacked them per se, but he just reminded everybody: "They've come a long ways! They're staying at our best hotels!" And remind them, of course, that you the taxpayer were paying for them.

He had lacerated them before they knew it! And a smile on their face. They don't know much about East Tennessee!

★ Ray Jenkins, *Terror of Tellico Plains: The Memoirs of Ray H. Jenkins*

In 1961 the law firm of Key & Lee (Clyde W. Key and McAfee Lee) and I were retained as defense counsel in an important income tax evasion case which attracted unusual public attention on a regional scale. The object or victim of the federal prosecution, however one regards the affair, was Cas Walker, wealthy chain grocer and Knoxville politician....

... Walker was a remarkable business success, buying up store after store or building new ones until he had supermarkets scattered around Knoxville and East Tennessee and beyond the state line. While all this was going on, the Internal Revenue Service, always greedy for money, had been watching the expansion with more than passing interest. Cas was indicted in the United States District Court for alleged income tax evasion....

... With the unwitting help of the government we made a martyr out of Cas. Kick a dog in the street and the public will turn against you. The government had a competent district attorney with an able staff here in Knoxville, but the government wanted blood. It sent down from Washington its top-flight lawyer on tax cases to help prosecute, and thus "overloaded" its staff. Certainly we were careful to select a jury of the common people, Cas's peers, who saw the farm boy, the coal miner, the benefactor of children and needy families, ridiculed and reviled as no other man within our recollection had ever been. The jury resented it.

We closed our proof by putting on the witness stand some of Knoxville's leading business and professional citizens. With these we went into detail as to how long they had known the defendant, what their association with

Cas Walker and U.S. Marshal Quarles, c. 1960. Printed by permission of the *Knoxville News Sentinel*.

him had been, and whether or not in their opinion he bore a reputation for truth and veracity. And finally was he entitled to full faith and credit on his oath, to which we got an emphatic answer that he was. . . .

. . . Throughout Cas's trial the government proceeded on the net worth theory, relying on figures and bookkeeping to show that the defendant's accumulation of wealth far exceeded the amount upon which he had paid income tax. We countered this by taking the position that this unlettered, unschooled, illiterate man knew nothing about bookkeeping, relied on others to prepare his returns, and that any discrepancies were honest mistakes.

Concluding, we made impassioned and emotional appeals to the jury. The verdict: "Not guilty."

Clyde Key, McAfee Lee, and I would be the first ones to admit some damaging evidence was proved against Cas Walker, but the government didn't have a chance against the ex–coal miner, merchant, politician, and benefactor. For our services he paid us a hundred thousand dollars without batting an eye.

Felonious Assault Charge

★ *Knoxville News-Sentinel*, June 11, 1971

"Cas Walker Charged After Woman Beaten"

City Councilman Cas Walker was charged Thursday at City Jail with felonious assault in the alleged manhandling of a 56-year-old woman while he was taping part of his television program at WBIR-TV (Channel 10) studio. The complainant was identified as Mrs. William F. (Mary) Tindell, 502 Atlantic Avenue. She was admitted to University Hospital with a broken elbow along with abrasions and other injuries, attendants said.

City Homicide Detectives Gene Morrell and Dave Gaddis said Mrs. Tindell told them she had gone to the studio early Thursday to talk with Councilman Walker about a church bond he was holding for her.

Mrs. Tindell said she had tried to see Walker Wednesday morning and afternoon about the bond but she could not contact him. She said she entered the studio where Walker was doing a live segment of his morning show and waited for him to finish. She told officers she walked to where he was seated and said she wanted to talk to him about the bond.

In a statement to police Mrs. Tindell said Walker jumped out of the chair, cursed at her and said, "you don't tell me what to do." Then she said "he struck me on the face several times, knocking me down." Mrs. Tindell also said Walker kicked her several times and grabbed her by the hair of the head and dragged her into another studio.

Police said she was unconscious when WBIR employees called City Patrolman Larry Everett to the scene. She was sent to the hospital and treated for injuries. WBIR-TV cameramen Walter McKinney Jr. and Steve Foster told Detectives Gaddis and Morrell that they saw Mrs. Tindell and Walker arguing but could not hear what was being said.

Councilman Walker later said Mrs. Tindell was "having a fit" and he was trying to get her out of the building when the incident occurred.

Concerning the incident Councilman Walker made a statement to a local radio news man that "the poor soul wanted to get on television and I would not let her, so I pulled her out by the hair of her head." Walker said there was no truth in the statement made by Mrs. Tindell concerning the alleged beating, but that he did lead her out of the studio by the hair "pretty rough."...

"No Hard Feelings," June 10, 1971. Walker makes amends with
Dave Gaddis and Gene Morrell who had arrested him for "felonious assault."
Printed by permission of the *Knoxville News Sentinel*.

According to Walker, Mrs. Tindell had created a disturbance in his office several days ago concerning the church bond. He said he had loaned Mrs. Tindell $100 on the bond several months ago and she had wanted it back because her husband had found out that it was missing and threatened to leave her.

Walker said she had slapped him in the mouth with her hand and she resisted him when he tried to calm her.

The councilman was released on his own recognizance from the City Jail. A City Court hearing is scheduled for 10 a.m. June 25.

★ Cas Walker, *My Life History*

A Sad Story

Here's something that I don't like to mention. It's about the woman that come into the television station and the manager had asked me to not let her get on the microphone anymore to do her Club Spots. He said, "You do

Mary H. Tindell with Robert Ritchie, July 2, 1971. Printed by permission of the *Knoxville News Sentinel*.

them for her or let Dan Bailey do it." This is where I ought to have told him to let someone else handle it. We had already had trouble with her in practically every store I had, I believe all of her boys had carried our paper over the years and they were fine boys. I am still for them. Her husband used to cut meat for me. I introduced her to him.

I knew Mary's folks real well and we were always friendly. She worked for me in the election. When I told Mary that I had orders not to let her on the microphone anymore, she said, "Hell, I don't care what they say. I'm going on." I said, "Not here." It was just about time for us to go on air. I started to push her over where she wouldn't been seen and she turned around and knocked three of my teeth out! I am not going to say anymore about it.

★ Betty Bean

Mary Tindell was a longtime fixture in Democratic Party politics, and she was pissed at Cas for, I think Cas had called her a bag woman—as opposed to a bag lady, I don't think that term was in use then—but he meant she was a crooked politician who carried money and delivered favors and bribes to people on behalf of certain politicos.

One morning, she came down to the studio in North Knoxville. She came to confront him. I mean, she just barged right in, they were on the air, and Cas was determined to kick her out of there and he literally did, and I think he hurt her.

He told me that—he kinda laughed—he said, "Well, she said I broke her ribs but her ribs weren't nowhere near where I kicked her!" And he used the term, he said, "I planted me a boot factory in her rear end!" He told me she fought like a bull; he claimed that she kicked his front teeth out. But I never read about that anywhere else, but he told me that years later; I don't know if that's true. I remember he said to me, "She was just an awful good woman, except she'd take these mad spells."

But I'd say she was extremely pissed. That's just my guess. I don't think she was exactly calm, you don't confront Cas Walker calm.

★ *Metro Pulse*, July 30th, 1998, by Betty Bean

[Cas said,] "She just rared back and hit me in the mouth and knocked out three of my teeth. She was strong as a bull. I started fighting her then, and Lord a' mercy, I just kicked her on out the door. Then, I went over to the jail and made bond. The next day, some of them tried to say I broke two of her ribs, but where I kicked her, her ribs wasn't near. I planted me a boot factory, and that never did cost me a cent. She was trespassing. She was an awful good woman except when she took these mad spells."

Insiders believed his plea bargain agreement included a promise not to run for reelection in 1971. Whatever the case, he retired from public office.

★ Unidentified Newspaper Clipping (ETHC)

"Walker, Butler Freed of Assault Charges"

The Knox County Grand Jury has declined to return felonious assault indictments against former City Councilman Cas Walker and former City Judge Jesse W. Butler. Mr. Walker was arrested and charged on June 10 in connection with the alleged beating of a 56-year old woman at the studios of WBIR-TV (Channel 10). . . .

. . . Millionare-grocer Walker was accused of beating and kicking Mrs. Mary Tindell, 502 Atlantic Ave., when she allegedly attempted to make an impromptu appearance on an early morning Walker-sponsored television program.

Testimony Secret

The controversial political figure was arrested after two WBIR employees, Steven Foster and Walker McKinney Jr., told city detectives they saw Mr. Walker hit, kick, and then drag Mrs. Tindell from the studio by her hair.

Although testimony before a grand jury is secret under state law, the News-Sentinel was told earlier that other law enforcement officers subsequently questioned six other witnesses who claimed the woman attacked Mr. Walker. They said the 68-year-old former councilman was actually attempting to restrain Mrs. Tindell who attacked him.

Church Bond Held

Mrs. Tindell did not appear before the grand jury. However, she sent a letter to the grand jury stating she was ill. Atty. Gen. Ronald Webster said the felonious assault charge was not acted upon because there was no evidence that a deadly weapon was used. The grand jury actually voted on an assault and battery charge.

At the time of his arrest, Mr. Walker talked candidly about the charge. In the salty mountain dialect that has marked his long political career, he said: "Well, all there was to it, this pore old soul come in there and wanted to get on television and I didn't let her get on. I led her out real nice—by the hair of the head."

Mrs. Tindell, the mother of Knox County Court Squire Billy Tindell, reportedly became upset because Walker officer workers would not return a church bond she had pledged in connection with a $100 loan. . . .

"How He Started Losing His Power"

★ Larry Mathis

What made Cas lose his power—you see, in the '40s and '50s and early '60s, Cas had all of the family watching. When the rock 'n' roll came out, these kids were up in high school: "Oh, look at that! Look at Elvis!" When that came along, they quit watching Cas.

Later on, Cas, you couldn't convict Cas hardly of anything. He'd get on TV and he'd "lamblast" somebody, and they wouldn't do nothing about it because they're afraid of his money, and they knew it wouldn't do no good. By the time these kids got up and started getting married, later on in the '80s, they had to serve jury duty and things like that. OK, they hadn't watched Cas.

Cas, he had the *Watchdog*, that paper, and he would maybe, "lamblast" this policeman or something, and tell them all he's doing is eating doughnuts and talking to the girls. He'd just bring out stuff like that. Whether it was true or not, that's the way he'd explain it.

So, what happened, I think how he started losing his power—this one policeman, it was in the *Watchdog*, he told about him or something. Well, that fellow, he balked on Cas and sued him. Well, he didn't have these old farmers from up in Claiborne County and places like that on the jury. These young people, they said, "Who's Cas Walker?"

So, whenever this policeman got judgment against him, well, the old cur dogs on the block said, "This bulldog down here has got him down, let's go down there and chew on him a little bit ourselves."

So, they started doing that. They started fighting back, because here they're filling up juries now.

And that's what really hurt country music for a long time, bluegrass especially. Because of rock 'n' roll and these kids, they flocked to that.

Well, kids didn't buy groceries. That's the reason Cas would never have no kind of music like that on his program, because kids don't buy groceries. Mom and Daddy buy groceries. So, he stuck to the kind of music that the mom and daddies watched. Then whenever it got to where these people were on juries, they didn't know who he was. And they started getting judgments against him, and I think that's where he probably lost a lot of his power and popularity....

★ *Knoxville News-Sentinel,* c. 1978

"Cooper Suit Says Watchdog Libeled"

Former city school board member Jack Cooper has filed a lawsuit in circuit court seeking $13 million in damages for alleged libelous statements made by Cas Walker in the giveaway *Watchdog* publication last fall. It is the largest such lawsuit ever filed in Knox County and one of the largest ever in the state. Cooper alleged that Walker became "disenchanted" with him while he served on the school board several years ago and began to print untruths and false accusations against him. According to Cooper, he was not a candidate in the 1977 school board race and did not participate in any campaign other than contributing money to several candidates running for office.

Cooper charged that Walker commenced printing libelous statements about him in the *Watchdog* . . . in June preceding the November election and continued printing such articles periodically. He charged the attacks against him and his family continued for about six months until Dec. 29, 1977. The first article, Cooper said, accused him of purchasing an expensive Cadillac shortly after his election in 1969 and using his position as a member of the school board for personal benefit. Later articles alleged that Cooper had spent $20,000 of a "slush fund" in running for the school board. Cooper also claimed the publication printed stories saying he had joined forces with a Knoxville liquor store operation in an attempt to defeat incumbent Julia Tucker last year. Tucker had beaten Cooper in 1973.

The articles also accuse Cooper of running "his campaign manager against Julia Tucker," the plaintiff alleged. Cooper said other allegations against him included that he was "trying to get on the school board through the back door" by supporting another candidate and that he had the support of the liquor and beer interests. Cooper said the paper made various references to his ties with the "whiskey operators" and the "booze crowd." He said one article expressed the opinion, "we don't see how anybody who is a good Christian could be for anybody the liquor crowd goes all out for." He claimed the *Watchdog* later printed what purported to be an apology, but the form of the apology was also libelous.

Another article, Cooper claimed, made inferences that he had participated in either making or receiving payoffs between building supply and lumber dealers and the school board in connection with building projects. . . . Cooper said Walker stated in another story he should expect to be attacked when he gets involved in politics. The plaintiff also alleged other articles accused his wife and daughter of improper acts and conduct. Cooper said he wrote letters to Walker and the Tennessee Valley Advertising Agency, owned by Walker and also a defendant, asking for retraction but none was forthcoming.

He said the pattern of attacks against him made it appear to the public that he was "immoral, dishonest, unethical, connected with mobsters and gangsters and a participant in a plan to take over certain governmental segments of the community for the purpose of distributing whiskey and other alcoholic beverages to the school children of his community." Cooper asked for $2 million in compensatory, and $8 million in punitive damages for himself; $500,000 compensatory and $1 million punitive damages each for his wife and daughter. Cas Walker Cash Stores, which is a primary distribution point for the *Watchdog*, was also made a defendant. Representing Cooper is attorney Keith McCord.

★ Bennie Wallen Jean

I know when I was working, before Kroger's came in, they tried to buy him out. And in my mind, I was thinking that was the thing to do and really, he was about to do it.

I was really getting worried myself 'cause I thought, "Will Kroger's keep his advertising agency?" And deep down, Mr. Walker's employees were worried about our own selves. We thought, "Kroger won't keep this advertising agency, we'll be out on the street."

But he decided that he loved his employees and he was afraid that Kroger's wouldn't keep them. He decided that he would just keep 'em, and they'd be one of his competitors. So that's what he did.

But the reason his stores declined was that he didn't bring up people that knew how to manage. Now his nephew Odell Cas Lane knew everything about the grocery business 'cause he started working with—Mr. Walker actually raised him. He knew all about it, but he got bone cancer and he died young. I came from Nashville for the funeral 'cause I liked him a lot.

So anyway, he died and then his head bookkeeper of all the stores—I don't know if she died or retired—but when all the structure and the backbones of his stores was not there, then I think he let one of his grandsons run it, be manager or something, and then he just didn't know beans about it. So anyway, they just started going downhill.

Cas and the Nursing Home

★ Betty Bean

So every year, I think it was probably on Thanksgiving day or maybe the day after, the *Journal* would start the Milk Fund drive. And we would try to compete with the *News-Sentinel* to raise money. We wouldn't admit that, but that's what we were doing. We'd have a story every day about some pitiful starving family, wheelchair tobacco farmers and whatever.

But the traditional kickoff story was a Cas Walker story, an interview with Cas. So I went out to the nursing home to see him and took a photographer with me. I was real skeptical about interviewing a guy who had been in a nursing home for however long who had Alzheimer's. And I was new at the paper, and I thought I got the short end of the stick on this one.

But he was utterly lucid and even charming. . . . For somebody who grew up in Knoxville, I'm practically a communist, I'm not mainstream—but for some reason Cas really liked me. Maybe he was just lonesome out there in the nursing home, although he'd kinda taken over the nursing home. He was leading people on nature walks and visitors—other residents' visitors—would come in to pay their respects to him. He was a celebrity there, so he probably wasn't too lonesome. He had his room decorated up with all his crap.

I really liked him and he was a great interview. He would tell me these wonderful stories and speak in paragraphs and then he would pause—and at that time, I'm just writing everything by hand. And he would wait, he'd give me time to finish the thought. He was a pro. And he was very polite and funny. Now he was always country; that tale that he spoke the queen's English, that's just bull hockey.

I came back and I said this guy does *not* have Alzheimer's. Well, some years later when I started doing these stories at *Metro Pulse* eight years later, O. C. Johnson, "Little Cas," his right-hand man, told me that Cas, it became clear that Cas did not—that he was misdiagnosed.

And he said that Cas was very, very angry about losing his business and also losing his city council seat. And his influence. The world was just passing him by, and he knew it. He was a smart guy, and he was very distraught over it. And it wasn't just money, it was everything he'd built was going away.

He said that Cas became violent and that you had to watch out for him. He said he carried a big ol' walking stick, a tall stick, and he said that he could hear him every morning, that stick hitting the floor: boom boom. And he could gauge how pissed Cas was, and apparently, he was always pissed.

O.C. believed that Cas had physically harmed Ginny. And she was a little tiny woman, and—now Cas loved her, he really did; I think he was not faithful to her but he loved her. I believe that she just had him committed as a danger to himself and her.

Cas did not leave the nursing home until she died; he left two or three weeks after she died.

Flowers for Virginia

★ Julia Rose

When I stayed at my grandmother's house we watched his show every morning and she shopped at his store. Always read his paper too. But the story I would like to share is how much he loved his wife, Virginia.

My senior year of high school (1980–81) I worked at Baker's Florist over on Western Avenue/Oak Ridge Highway. Cas had a standing order for us to deliver flowers to his wife every week on Tuesdays. He would come in periodically and fill out six or seven of the cards for us to attach to the flowers and put them in the envelopes. He always had us deliver seasonal appropriate bouquets. She always acted surprised and complimented the flowers. She invited me in for glass of lemonade or tea and tipped me a dollar every week. No matter what else the Old Coon Hunter was, he was a man who loved his wife. My boss said this had gone on for years.

★ Bo Pierce

Virginia Walker had more physical ailments, hips and knees and stuff, where Cas was diagnosed with Alzheimer's, mental stuff.

When Miss Virginia passed away a few years later, Cas escapes. He gets out, and of course he's telling everybody they had him misdiagnosed; it was medications and stuff. And for a fact, he did some commercials after that, coming out for some car dealers on Clinton Highway. It was just like twenty years earlier, there's Cas out there on TV!

And then his good friend David West, at Ciderville Music, was basically the band leader for the live band he had on his morning show. Cas would go out to Ciderville, and he was a rock star out there. He'd sit on Friday and Saturday nights—when they did a live music show—he'd sit out there and sign autographs and talk about Supraderm Salve.

Ciderville is like a museum. "That's the chair he sat in!" David's got a lot of the set from WBIR and WATE—it's a museum out there.

Cas and Virginia "Ginny" Walker, date unknown.
Printed by permission of the *Knoxville News Sentinel*.

★ *Metro Pulse*, July 30, 1998, by Betty Bean (Excerpt)

Fall of an Empire

Wilma June died in 1979. Cas' nephew and foster son, Odell Cas Lane, who worked in the business and served in the State Legislature, died as well. Cas Walker was desolate. His health began to fail and so did his business. Bit by bit, he was shorn of everything that was important to him. By 1984, he was living in a home with a diagnosis of Alzheimer's.

The Cas Walker Supermarkets were taken over by his heirs, who changed the name of the chain to Food Plus. By 1985, Food Plus was in receivership, and Walker told the *News-Sentinel* that he wanted to come out of retirement to salvage his business. "You can't smile at your funeral."

By 1987, his mind was clear and his doctors were admitting that he had been misdiagnosed. Peggy Savage, administrator of the nursing home where he was living, said Walker had been suffering from stress and depression complicated by overmedication. She said he had taken the Alzheimer's patients at the home into his care, taking them for walks and trying to cheer them up.

"He is just the most loving, generous person. He is a real force for good here," she told the *Knoxville Journal* that December. The following December, Walker, back home, gave his annual Milk Fund interview to the *Journal*—but he was lacking the old fire.

"I lost Ginny you know," he said. "She died at 5 minutes to 7 on Saturday morning. November 3rd. If she'd lived till the next day, we'd have lived together 62 years. . . . It'll be an awful hard Christmas without her."

And Today . . .

There's a welcome mat with a raccoon on it at the front door of the modest Gaston Avenue homeplace he never left, even when he was the richest man in town. He is lying there on a hospital bed in the living room, heart monitor attached, being fussed over by three women who call him Dadaw.

His nurse, Blanche Breeden, has known him for most of her 62 years and likes to joke that she was his original Blanche, long before Dolly Parton. He hasn't spoken for three months. That voice—the one that sounds like somebody scraped out his vocal cords and replaced them with rusty ten-penny nails—is still.

He is bedfast, locked inside a body that failed him two years ago on his 94th birthday, as Blanche was taking him out to David West's Music Barn for a party in his honor. "He walked out of the house out to the car, opened up the car door, got in and sat down. Right in front of the Wal-Mart on Clinton Highway he just quit talking, and that's not like Mr. Walker. He had a seizure of some kind. I don't know what happened to him and the doctors don't know what happened to him."

He communicates by blinking his eyes. Blanche translates. The old man whose colorful life overflows and spills out of fat brown envelopes in a library drawer downtown has approved a "Do not resuscitate" order.

Walker doesn't make it out to Homecoming at the Museum of Appalachia anymore, but museum director John Rice Irwin says when he did, he caused the most stir of any celebrity who was ever there.

"People just wanted to touch him, see him, talk to him," he says. "Almost everybody who talks about Cas Walker talks about what they've heard other people say about him. I'd always heard everything he did was self-serving. But when we started the Homecoming 19 years ago, I asked him to promote it. And he took this thing up and promoted it every morning instead of selling groceries. He let us come on as much as we wanted to for years. I kept thinking this wasn't consistent with the popular portrayal of the man."

Asked if he likes Walker, Irwin thinks a minute, then recalls something John C. Calhoun said about Henry Clay:

"He said, 'No, I don't like Henry Clay. He's devious and he's treacherous and you can't trust him. I don't like Henry Clay—I love him.'

"And I love Cas Walker."

★ *Knoxville Journal,* October 5, 1988

"Putting End to Rumors Will Make Walker's Day" by Betty Bean

MARYVILLE—Thursday is Cas Walker Day at the Museum of Appalachia's Tennessee Fall Homecoming, and Knoxville's most famous retired grocer-politician will be there to clear up some rumors.

Walker, 85, has been a resident of the Colonial Heights Nursing Home in Maryville for the past 2½ years. He says he is looking forward to going out to the museum in Norris so he can see old friends and let them know that he's doing well. "They tried to say that I had Alzheimer's disease, but it turned out that what I did have was a nervous breakdown," Walker said Tuesday.

"And then I came out of Asbury Acres (a convalescent home in Blount County), and I was working day and night trying to get my business back in shape. . . . And I just wore out. Old age caught up with me."

Colonial Heights administrator Dr. Peggy Savage says Walker may be correct in his self-diagnosis. She said he is thriving in the stress-free environment of the home. "I think you could safely say be believes he has been misdiagnosed," Savage said. "And his present level of functioning indicates that could easily have been the case."

". . . He was under so much stress when he got here that he didn't know up from down, inside from out. He was suffering from stress and depression, but he improved so much in his first six months here that he's like a different person now."

Walker said he has great sympathy with the Alzheimer's patients at the home, and Savage reported that he has taken a group of them under his wing, going for twice-daily walks with them and generally trying to cheer them up.

"He is just the most loving, generous person. He is a real force for good here," she said.

Walker, who in his political heyday rarely heard himself described as "a force for good," keeps up with the news and holds strong opinions on a broad range of issues. . . .

Museum of Appalachia founder John Rice Irwin said the day dedicated to Cas Walker will be an important part of the ninth annual Homecoming celebration. "Cas Walker is undoubtedly the best-known and most controversial East Tennessee politician since Parson Brownlow after the Civil War. He is part of our heritage. He started many of the people who have become stars in the type of music that many of us were ashamed of.

"There was a time when I thought he was a money-grabbing, penny-pinching old Scrooge, and then he spent thousands of dollars worth of airtime plugging this museum, and the same thing with the Milk Fund. He had nothing at all to gain.

"And it just seems fitting to honor a person who is credited for helping so many people make good."

Last Days

★ Bradley Reeves

For several years, I had been urged by a family member living in Walker's North Hills neighborhood to just stop by and have a chat with him, that Cas loved visitors, and talking about the old days.

Cas Walker was just part of growing up in Knoxville, part of the fabric. He was always on television, in the news, and as children, we were fascinated by the large painted yellow footprints that led up the sidewalks and into his grocery stores. As an adult, I wanted to meet this man that played such a large role in Knoxville history.

I kept putting off a visit, until one summer afternoon, knowing his advanced age, and the fact that I was moving from Knoxville to attend film school in a few weeks, I decided this might be my last chance. I managed to talk a few others into going, and off we went to meet the legendary Cas Walker!

We knocked on the door at the Gaston Avenue home, and were received by a friendly caretaker who told us that Cas was in, and we could come inside to see him for a fee of $5.00 each. I paid the fee for two of us, which the nurse promptly placed in her apron pocket, next to a large pack of Winston Red cigarettes.

Things became more unsettling as we were led through a living room sparsely decorated in what appeared to be 1950s-era furniture. I spotted a vintage television playing an old movie in the background, and I'm fairly certain it was an older black and white model, still in use in 1998!

The caretaker led us into the front bedroom, and there he was, laying in a bed with his eyes open, seemingly aware of both his visitors and surroundings. The caretaker then informed us that Cas could not speak, and at that point, all of us realized we were in a seriously awkward moment, but that it was too late to turn back! The nurse seemed to know a lot about Cas, holding up his hand, and telling us about how his crooked finger was bitten off in a fight and reattached, but Walker managed to chew the other fellow's ear off. About that time, I noticed the frozen-in-shock look on the face of the young lady who accompanied us.

The caretaker told some other stories, of which I can't recall, as I was too busy trying to figure out a way to gracefully make our way out of there.

So I told Cas, and I'm pretty sure he was listening, and that he understood, that I appreciated him, and all that he had accomplished. I appreciated his history, and that it meant a lot to me personally to finally meet him. I then thanked him, and we hurriedly left what seemed to be a living museum. Cas passed away shortly thereafter.

★ Rowdy Cope

The day before he died, I was there. I went in just goofing off and saying "hi" to him. I took my guitar, and you know what his favorite song was? "You Can Be a Millionaire with Me." Actually, he paid for Pappy Gube Beaver to record that song on RCA—"You Can Be a Millionaire with Me."

He had 8.5 million when he passed on.

Cas Walker late in life, date unknown.
Printed by permission of the *Knoxville News Sentinel*.

EPILOGUE

The Legacy of Cas Walker

Decades after his death, Cas Walker still fascinates many East Tennesseans. Some still remember brief encounters or seeing Cas from a distance during one of his promotions. Others who lived and worked with him treasure stories that reflect his impact on their lives. And many tell a set of legends, mostly true, that make up a central part of Knoxville's urban folklore. Undoubtedly, Cas Walker had an effect on the city of Knoxville and its residents in the twentieth century, one that still lingers today. But the question remains as to what exactly that effect was. Would Knoxville have remained a country town if left up to Cas Walker? Many of those who knew Cas Walker personally reminisced about his place in the city's history. This epilogue gathers these opinions into one place where readers can parse for themselves the role of this "hillbilly colossus" in the history of East Tennessee.

"Everybody Had a Cas Walker Story"

★ David Correll

Cas was a smart business man but he also loved to help people that needed help. He kept food on many people's table that could not afford to buy food. He gave people food and money that had lost their jobs and had a family to feed. He gave people that needed clothing. He was a very generous man that helped many people get started in a career.

★ David West

Well, everybody had a Cas Walker story because he'd done something for everybody. He either fired you, or hired you; he'd done something good, he didn't do nothing bad to you.

But he didn't like hoodlums, he didn't like crooked politicians, he didn't like dog thieves. And if you was wrong, he'd look you in the eye and say, "You're no good"—just like that!

He didn't think. He'd say, "Well, you need to straighten up 'cause you ain't no good. You could be but you're not."

You knew he was Cas Walker.

They either loved him or hated him. The people who hated him had a bad trail. I watched every one of them, I watched people all my life that got to work with him. Anybody that had something bad to say about him, I checked them out, and their trail was very flimsy. It was a crooked path of crooks.

★ Victor Ashe

He was colorful. He was unique. I don't know many other communities that had someone quite like him.

He had never gotten too big for his britches; he was still the Cas they'd always known, or at least pretended to be. And I think people believed that.

You know, his final days, he lived in very modest home right off Broadway in North Knoxville. It wasn't impoverished, it wasn't a slum, it wasn't trashy, but it was at best, lower-middle income. Nothing bad about it, but it certainly didn't connote prosperity or great business success, or that he was a millionaire.

I don't know what he was in his older years, but there was a time when he would've been a millionaire, I think. But he was never accepted by the "proper people" of the community. He wasn't a person that a well-to-do businessperson would invite to his home. He would do business with him, but it would be in a business setting. He certainly never bothered with the Cherokee Country Club—wouldn't have gotten in. He wouldn't have wanted to be in. He would ridicule that. That would have no interest to him.

★ Carl Warner

He became a multimillionaire, I know. For example, even though my job was editor of the *Watchdog*, I'd be at the office, and he said, "Carl, do something for me. Take this down to my bank and deposit it."

He had a thing about his personal account; it had to have a million dollars in it. And anytime he would get a notice from his bank that was below a million, he'd give me a check from another account to run down and put it in his bank account so it would get back up to a million. I did that several times, during the time I was working for him. Strange, but that was Cas.

★ Larry Mathis

He had an old Rambler that he drove all the time. He wouldn't let a Cadillac sit in his yard for nothing. In 1957, maybe, Dunn and Bradstreet at that time rated him at $13 million. In '57, that's a lot of money. But you'd never know.

We used to go to the stores when they'd have a new opening, up in, say, he had one up in Corbin, Kentucky. We'd go up there, he'd have six or eight of us go up there and play, all day. Grand opening. A promotion. Something like that.

I've seen people come up wearing suits and go to talking to him. I have literally seen this. He'd see an old boy over there in overalls, and he'd just walk off from that fellow in the suit and go over there and all laughing and shaking hands and everything. That was the kind of people he catered to. Cas was always for the old country fellow. He was always that. Because that's what he was.

★ Bradley Reeves

He was a prominent East Tennessean—he was himself, and he wasn't dealing with what I could say, the snotty upper-crust. *Those* folks. There's a lot to be said for that; that's why I like him, because he was a rebel, and he did it his way (with apologies to Mr. Sinatra). He made a success out of himself. At one point, he had so much power, he didn't care; he could speak his mind. How many people can do that? It must be very refreshing.

Now, I'm not saying he was an angel. He did some nasty stuff, but gosh, most people in high places have.

I'm neutral on Cas; I like him, I like the thought of him, but I also see the other side. People say, "Oh, well, he held this town back." I think this town held itself back, but he kind of voiced that, he was the mouthpiece. He was against it; they don't like change, that old-school fear of change and wanting to do something different.

He's a fascinating guy. Knoxville's actually lucky to have a character like that in a lot of ways. But he also brings about memories of an unkinder and politically corrupt era.

So I don't know. Again, I'm neutral, which is a weird place to be in.

★ Ben Walker

Oh, he was a bare-knuckle politician. He had a lot of power in Knoxville, and everybody knew, most people did not cross him because they couldn't win. Listen, he took what he had—no education, but he had brains evidently, and he used them and got what all politicians are trying to get. You just think about it: he did what all of them are trying to get, which was fame and money. That's what all of them are after. I know that from being seventy-nine years old.

★ Julia Tucker

I have found that politicians and powerful people have a feeling of superiority, and they're unable to . . . their passion and their verve is almost impossible to satiate. They just want more, and it becomes a feeling that "I can do this, I can do more." I've seen it locally, and I see it nationwide now, too. And the feeling of power is absolutely intoxicating. And corrupting. It is.

He speaks for the common man, the people that don't have a voice, and also the people that are superior and kind of say, "Well, ol' Cas, he was OK. He said a lot of things, but he was OK." And it's a perverse thing that he is revered, but it's OK. It's OK that he is, but people don't know who he really was.

They didn't know those things, and actually I guess they didn't need to know, because let them have their dream of who Cas was.

Everybody has their feet of clay, but his feet of clay went up to his neck.

★ Jack Wiedemann

I don't know that his legacy is what he would want it to be. There are people that hated Cas as much as he hated them. He was divisive. I'm sure he did some good for Knoxville, but if he had had his way, Knoxville would be still a country town.

★ Jack Sharp

A lot of people say he was holding Knoxville back. And maybe he did at the time. But overall, it turned out good. Because it gave people time, made them think. Maybe some of these businesspeople back then thought, "Well, he might be a little right," or, "We better be a little cautious."

Because if you got your own way and nobody's questioning it, there's no telling what you'll come up with, if you've got a straight shot.

And other people argue that, too: "If it's a good idea and good for everybody, why not do it, Jack?"

But you gotta have a bump in the road, and he was the bump. He might have been a big boulder.

★ Randy Tyree

I have thought about—this is just in my own mind—I wonder, I think Cas is due a lot of legitimacy for his role in our history, for making good things happen simply because he would be against those things, and he would make the rest of us that was for them get off our duffs and say, "We're gonna make this happen."

I know that was relevant during the World's Fair, because it was sort of like, "If Cas is agin' it, we gotta be for it."

And Cas was, "If they're for it, I'm agin' it."

More than anything else—and I'm by no stretch a historian, but I did minor in it in college, and I love it as just a student of history. Take thirty years, and in our community, in our politics, in our attitudes, we have been and continue to be progressive, and we're becoming more progressive every day. Because we're breaking down so many of those old barriers.

★ Bradley Reeves

What strikes me is—whether he was around for so long, or whether it was because he was so popular—is how his legacy is so enduring. I spoke with a lady two weeks ago. I called her in West Virginia. She used to live in Knoxville, moved away decades ago. We were taking about Knoxville; this was totally unrelated to Cas Walker, but somehow his name got brought up, and immediately she started singing his theme song—"Pick up the morning paper"—well, that's all I remember. But she started singing it, eighty years old, on the phone.

There was a time I was in Jacksonville Florida. I was in an antique store, the guy said, "Where you from, fellow?

I said, "Knoxville, Tennessee."

He said, "Oooohh, Cas Walker!" He never lived here, but he knew!

The guy's reach is still astounding. I love the fact that he's such an East Tennessee icon. I realize that he could probably be a bastard, or if he didn't like you, he could make your life hell.

★ *Knoxville News-Sentinel,* August 29, 1998

"There Wasn't Much Middle of the Road About Cas Walker" by Sam Venable

There's a sure-fire test to determine if someone is a native Knoxvillian of long standing, and it has nothing to do with knowledge of landmarks or recall of ancient Vol football scores.

Just ask 'em to "do Cas."

If they wrinkle their brow and say, "Do what?" you are dealing with an import. Give them a Perrier and send them back to Pittsburgh.

If, however, they lower their voice an octave and cough out a gravelly, "Say, friends and neighbors, we got this Blue Band coffee for 69 cent a pound," you are talking to the genuine article.

Love him or hate him, Cas Walker, who died Friday at 96, was the genuine article for Knoxville. Although his role had greatly diminished over the last 15 to 20 years, he was a major player in this territory for the better part of half a century.

He was a businessman who raked in millions with a chain of grocery stores. He was a politician who made friends and enemies by being an "aginer"—"agin" just about any new concept or project that came down the pike. He was an entertainer who launched the careers of any number of country music stars. He was a shameless newspaper publisher who ruthlessly attacked anyone who dared cross his path.

But I like to remember him as Knoxville's lovable rogue. No matter what the situation or issue, Cas Walker always had an answer and an opinion. No matter how outlandish or reasonable his stance happened to appear, no matter if you wanted to laugh or to cry, all could be explained by simply saying, "That's just Cas."

Cas handled the truth to fit the occasion. He could be honest with one breath and hoodwink with the next. Many of his sales techniques were as hilarious as they were fraudulent.

Lynn Leopper, a retired WBIR-TV executive, directed Walker's "Farm and Home Hour" between 1959 and 1964. He recalled the morning Cas was doing a live commercial and picked up the wrong item.

"Back in those days of black-and-white television, anything on the set that was real shiny would show up as black on your TV at home," he explained. "We used a commercial spray to tone it down. Just before one broadcast, one of the floor men was spraying some of the items and set his can down in the middle of Cas' groceries. I guess the guy got distracted by something else. Anyhow, the can wound up in the commercial."

No problem. Cas started down the line in front of the camera, shilling coffee, bread, meat and other foodstuffs, when his gnarled fingers stopped.

"Cas picked up that can, turned it over and said, 'Neighbors, we got this DuPont dullin' spray. I can't remember how much we're askin' for it, but I know we sold a carload of it last week at the North Central store,' and went right on, just like that was part of the script."

Larry Mathis played banjo on the show from 1959 until 1970 and can spit out Cas tales like seeds from one of those "thumpin'-good" watermelons the grocer used to advertise.

"The river washed into his store in Pennington Gap (Va.) one day and got into a bunch of overalls," recalled Mathis. "Cas went on the air that mornin' and announced he was havin' a big flood sale on overalls up there. Well, after about an hour, the store manager in Pennington Gap called and told Cas he'd sold plumb out. Cas immediately sent a man out to his other stores and told him to round up all the overalls and drive 'em to Pennington Gap fast as he could. He also told him to throw 'em in a big pile and hose 'em down, just like they'd been flooded."

Sometimes he even fooled himself.

"Cas always kept 40 or 50 coon dogs in his kennel," Mathis said. "One day on TV, he started talking about some he had for sale.

"He started describing this one particular red bone. Said it had a good mouth and was a good cold-trailer and wouldn't run deer or rabbits. Cas just kept goin' on and on about what a fine dog this was when he looked at the camera and said, 'Wait a minute! I've always wanted a dog like this! This 'un ain't for sale.'"

"We Just Can't Shake Cas"

★ *Metro Pulse*, June 3, 2009

"Cas Walker, Hillbilly Colossus: Why the Legends of Ornery Grocer-Politician Cas Walker Still Haunt Knoxville" by Betty Bean

On a hot afternoon in late September 1998, I was sitting in the back seat of Johnny Strange's Cadillac in the parking lot of Mynatt's Funeral Home. Bobby Toole was riding shotgun and we were five or six cars back from the hearse that would carry Cas Walker's body across town to South Knoxville to be buried in Woodlawn Cemetery next to his wife, Virginia. Bobby and Johnny were two of Cas's closest friends, and they'd kindly offered me a ride.

Bobby "Coaldaddy" Toole was one of the original keepers of the flame, a job he took on while Cas was still alive. Back when I worked for the *Knoxville Journal*, I'd been instructed to be on the lookout for this quintessential Friend of Cas, because he was always up to no good. He lived up on Black Oak Ridge in C. H. Butcher's mansion, "Butch View," which he bought at auction after the Butcher banking empire went under. He was a notorious old-timey ward-heeling political boss who had a shock of white hair, shaggy black eyebrows and an unlit stogie that he chewed until cigar juice dribbled down the front of his shirt.

It was his habit to call everybody—even other men—"honey," and he'd stuck with Cas through good times and bad. After Cas got sprung from the nursing home where Ginny had stashed him when he was misdiagnosed with Alzheimer's, Bobby and his running buddy, KPD detective Don Wiser, would pick him up at his Gaston Avenue home and take him riding in one of Bobby's old police cruisers (also bought at auction). Some Tuesday evenings they'd take him downtown so he could stand up at City Council and denounce Victor Ashe, which always perked Cas up.

Cas had served on City Council longer than I'd been alive, and had been among the first to grasp the power of television not only for selling stuff but for fighting off fluoridation, metro government, bad check writers, shoplifters, dog thieves, civic improvements of any sort, and police officers who hung around and drank coffee in establishments other than his own. This hillbilly colossus lived to be 96 and bestrode the Knoxville landscape for nearly 70 years—an East Tennessee version of Huey Long (minus, of course, the Kingfish's massive building program and spectacular exit). His domination of Knoxville's politics, business and media was so complete that his name remains a household word for most any East Tennessean over the age of 35 or so.

My younger self would have been surprised to see my middle-aged self riding in his funeral procession, in part because my generation suspected that Cas Walker would never die, but mostly because I never figured I'd care if he did. East Tennessee Baby Boomers were raised on thumpin' good watermelons and bad Cas Walker jokes (e.g. 'What happened when Cas Walker's caught on fire? He grabbed his meat and beat it.'). We mocked his gravelly voice—"Say, Neighbors"— and we repeated stories about him putting formaldehyde in his hamburger. We looked down our rock 'n' roll noses at his countrified ways, but we figured he'd be right there on the TV at the end of world, flogging Blue Band Coffee and Mrs. Paul's Fish Sticks and having little blond-headed cloggers flouncing around in big skirts and showing their panties, embarrassing the living crap out of us when our cousins would come from Connecticut and Texas to visit.

I hadn't known any of them in their heyday, and by the time Cas died, Johnny was just a pretty nice guy who offered me a ride in his Cadillac and Bobby was a living relic of old time city politics and a crazy old coot with a million stories, maybe a quarter of which were true.

We'd just sat through a surprisingly brain-numbing service that wasn't even livened up by the presence of the Rev. J. Bazzel and Mrs. Mull (at least that's what I like to say since I recall so little of it). I was glad when it was over.

Cas had outlived most of his friends and colleagues, and the funeral procession wasn't near as long as it should have been, but I was keenly aware that this was a historic event, so, as we started off down Broadway, I made a point of counting landmarks along the way. The first one didn't involve Cas at all, but is too good a story not to tell and happened on a spot down in front of what Fountain Citians call the Hill's shopping center where one of Bobby's employees was attempting to drive a giant excavator called a Gradall down the road and plowed into an innocent motorist.

Wiser remembers the incident well:

"Bobby had an old Gradall (an oversized truck equipped with a huge hydraulic excavating bucket) he'd bought from the city, and he'd dug out the side of Black Oak Ridge where he was wanting to put him in a Quonset hut. He liked Quonset huts."

A lot of people thought C. H. and Shirley Butcher had turned their once-stately mansion into the godawfulest white trash wet dream imaginable, but they couldn't compare to Bobby, who collected heavy equipment and old police cruisers and liked to park junked cars on the tennis court. There came a time when Bobby decided to move the Gradall out to Andrew Johnson Highway, and unaware that his mechanic had disconnected the air brakes, he got a guy called Long John to drive it.

"They started down the hill," Wiser says, "Long John right in back of Bobby, old Long John a'blowin' that horn. Bobby got to the bottom of the hill and turned right on Broadway with old Long John speeding up and Bobby speeding up and they're going faster and faster with old Long John hittin' that brake and blowin' the horn and finally Bobby got out from in front of him and Long John went on down the road and hit a man in the oncoming lane right in front of Hill's."

Another block south on Broadway is the cutoff to Old Broadway where the Fountain City Cas Walker's store used to be. My Granddaddy, Ralph Bean, aka the Singing Mailman, used to take me in there when I was little, and I still remember the smell of overripe bananas and decaying meat, a world removed from the cinnamon bun and stargazers ambiance of a modern-day Fresh Market. That was where Cas caught my brother, John "LeRoy Mercer" Bean, scooping up an armload of Watchdogs to give to his friends to study. He told Cas he was taking them to shut-ins at the nursing home.

The next surviving landmark was Eddie's Auto Parts on our left, which still sits on the little stub of Walker Boulevard that survived the construction of I-640. Eddie Harvey bought a couple of lots from Cas to build his iconic store. Some years later, Eddie embellished it with a sign from the Italian Pavilion at the World's Fair.

A mile or so down the road we passed the intersection of Edgewood where you turn off to go to the WBIR TV station. That's where Cas got into a fight with a politically active Democrat named Mary Tindell (mother of former County Commissioner Billy Tindell, grandmother of state Rep. Harry Tindell) when she came down during the Farm & Home Hour studio one morning to confront him about some political something or other and he booted her out the door, literally. A lot of people think the resulting assault charge was enough to leverage him out of running for re-election to

City Council, something the silk-stocking crowd had been wishing would happen for decades....

... My second husband had, for a time, been the news reader on the Farm & Home Hour, and he'd come home with outrageous stories about the goings-on there, like the time Cas pulled a little curved stick that appeared to be made of ivory out of his pocket.

"What's that?" the Ex asked. "A coon pecker," Cas said.

It was not until the age of Google that I decided this was a plausible tale, since not believing the Ex was always a prudent default position. I did, kind of, believe the story about "peter peppers," the penis-shaped red peppers that ukulele player Honey Wilds allegedly grew in his garden, but that was after I saw Cas showing off some tubular produce he kept calling "Honey's peppers" one morning. They were a salty bunch.

A few miles south, we rolled into the Western Avenue intersection at the L&N Station where Broadway becomes Henley. The old City Hall on the left is where Cas made Knoxville a laughing stock in the '50s by getting into a fistfight with fellow City Councilman J. S. Cooper during a council meeting. A Journal photographer got a good shot of the action, and the picture ended up in Life Magazine. Although this is an indivisible part of his legend, Cas told me that the whole thing was "a put-up deal" that he'd faked.

The Sunsphere loomed on the right a block south, a reminder of how Cas fought the 1982 World's Fair with all his waning power. And although the fair was pretty much a hell of a party, the collapse of the Butcher banking empire that was its aftermath surpassed even Cas's dire predictions. But he was out of office by then and people had pretty much quit listening to him, although the Farm & Home Hour did continue until March 30, 1983.

The gigantic convention center that sits in front of the Sunsphere was just a gleam in Victor Ashe's eye by the time Cas died, but it's not hard to imagine what he would have had to say about that money pit if he'd been around when it was built.

Another block south on the left was the intersection of Main Street on the way to the City County Building, which, Cas, of course, opposed, mostly because he opposed anything new, but specifically because he worried that it would lead to metro government, fluoridated water, and probably godless communism.

We got on the Henley Bridge and crossed the Tennessee River (Cas would never have called it Ft. Loudoun Lake) into South Knoxville. Over on the right, down on the Vestal side of Chapman Highway, stood the dumpy little building that used to be his corporate headquarters. He had a snarly stuffed raccoon in the reception area along with an equally mean-looking, life-sized painting of himself. There was a desk for a secretary, but it was never occupied. Visitors just looked for his car (generally a Nash Rambler that he'd take the back seat out of so he could haul his coon dogs around), and went on in and hollered for him.

A block south, in a spot at the base of Ft. Dickerson where the kudzu threatens to cover everything in its path, we passed by what used to be Cas Walker's Chapman Highway Supermarket—probably the biggest store in the whole chain. Disc Exchange and some other businesses are there now, and they draw a pretty different clientele than the customers who used to Stop, Shop and Save at the Sign of the Shears. Maybe it was my imagination, but I thought I could make out that patched-up spot in the parking lot where Cas buried Digger O'Dell alive in 1960 as a unique promotional event. I'm pretty sure I went to see Digger one Sunday when I went home from First Methodist Church with my best friend Sylvia Stout, who lived over in Lindbergh Forest a couple blocks away. Cas figured that was his second-best publicity stunt, surpassed only by giving away copies of Elvis Presley's will with $10 grocery orders.

It wasn't far from there to the south end of Woodlawn, and we pulled into the front part of the old cemetery where an open grave next to [Ginny's] awaited. Granddaddy Bean and my brother John are buried there, too, up on the hill overlooking the Walker plot. Granddaddy bought his plots from a guy named Roe Ford, who sang in the Dixie Gems quartet with him. Maybe Cas knew Roe. I bet he got a deal.

We all piled out of our cars and gathered at the graveside for a brief final prayer service. Bobby, Johnny and I were among the last to leave, and just before we did, Bobby walked over to the casket, which was sitting on a swatch of artificial turf while the gravediggers waited for us to leave. He put his hand on the smooth wood and gave the benediction: "He was a good son of a bitch."

We got back into the Caddy and Johnny and Bobby took me back to Fountain City and dropped me off at Mynatt's. On my way home, I wondered what it was going to be like in a Cas Walker–free world.

But going on 11 years after his death, he's still with us. Cas Walker lives not only in our oral tradition, but in 232,000 Google hits, dozens of YouTube clips and on the Dolly Parton Heartsongs album where she sings his Farm & Home Hour theme song just like she used to do when she was on his radio show as a kid. Precocious dirty trickster Tyler Harber, a Farragut High School junior when Cas died, appropriated Cas's name for an infamous website set up to punish Mayor Mike Ragsdale's political enemies a few years back. My son the lawyer has a photograph of the "Three Best Things in the World—watermelon, possum and Cas Walker" sign hanging in his San Diego home.

Call it the mystic chords of memory or shared tribal experience, but no matter how far we travel, we just can't shake Cas, and we probably can't even tell you exactly why, any more than we can say why we like our tea sweet and our chicken fried. It's an East Tennessee thing, and unless you can answer me with the second line of the Farm & Home Hour theme song when I sing "Pick up the morning paper when it hits the street," you just wouldn't understand.

Postscript

★ Bruce Wheeler

Well, my first encounter with Cas Walker, I was asked to give a presentation to the East Tennessee History Group about Cas Walker. Mike McDonald and I were working on a book at the time about Knoxville history. We were there and the room was filled, because Walker would fill any room.

And as we finished the door in the back opened and in came Cas Walker. At one time, he had little tie-tacks with brass shears, since his thing was cutting prices. He was handing them out as he came down the center aisle.

And then someone asked him, "Well, do you have any comments about this?"

He said, "Yes, I do. Well, I'm sure that these men are loved by their mothers and are good to their mothers, but they've got a lot of this wrong."

He wasn't in the room, so I couldn't tell what he had overheard. But I've always had the suspicion—and now I can't prove it, because the people who would tell me are no longer living—that he really had invented a good part of his autobiography.

And even those people now who want to get at the real Cas Walker have accepted a lot of what he said.

CONTRIBUTORS

VICTOR ASHE served as mayor of Knoxville from 1987 to 2003. While he did not work alongside Cas Walker, his tenure as mayor ushered Knoxville into the post-Walker age.

As a journalist for the *Knoxville Journal, Metro Pulse,* and the *Shopper,* BETTY BEAN interviewed and profiled Cas Walker many times. Her work frames the narrative of this book.

ROBERT "BOB" BOOKER served as a State Representative from East Tennessee from 1969 to 1972, authored several books, and has a recurring history column in the *Knoxville News Sentinel.* As a leader in the sit-in movement in Knoxville, he knew Walker during the years when the city was forced to deal with the demand for African-American civil rights.

JAMES "JIM" BRAGG is Cas Walker's nephew. He has worked as a dentist in East Tennessee and enjoys recalling stories from his childhood about his one-of-a-kind uncle.

ROWDY COPE—also known as "Preacher"—worked as a horse trainer for Cas. Rowdy spent much of his life with Walker as a confidant and longtime friend.

BECKY ORANGE DWARSHIUS worked at the nursing home where Cas spent a few years in the late 1980s. Still a resident of East Tennessee, Becky remembers Cas fondly.

As a former secretary at the Tennessee Valley Advertising Agency, BENNIE WALLEN JEAN was at the center of Cas's marketing empire for nearly two decades.

ROBERT "BOB" LUTTRELL worked as an illustrator for the *Knoxville News Sentinel* and is a proud World War II veteran. He recalls what it was like to do business with Cas.

LARRY MATHIS played banjo on Cas's "Farm and Home Hour." He accompanied Dolly Parton's early performances, entertained at the Grand Ole Opry for years, and remains a respected musician today.

One of BO PIERCE's first professional jobs was with the Knox County Housing Authority. There he met Cas Walker and navigated public housing issues for the county.

BRADLEY REEVES created the Tennessee Archive of Moving Image and Sound [TAMIS], which operates in the East Tennessee History Center. He continues to gather rare recordings through his new organization, Cinegraphic Archives and Preservation.

JACK SHARP served as a city councilman in Knoxville from 1976 to 2003. His family has a long history in Knoxville politics, which makes him a keen observer of Walker's accomplishments.

JULIA TUCKER served as the first female city school board chair in the early 1980s. She and Cas had a complex relationship, one that erupted in a courtroom drama well covered in the local media.

RANDY TYREE served as Knoxville's police chief before becoming the youngest mayor ever elected in Knoxville (1976-1983). He tells of how Cas helped his election and of the grocer's initial misgivings about the World's Fair.

BEN H. WALKER is a nephew of Cas Walker. He worked at Cas's grocery stores in his youth and today defends his colorful uncle's good name.

For three years, CARL WARNER edited Cas Walker's newspaper the *Watchdog*. He recalls what it was like to wrangle Cas's opinions into print without getting sued.

DAVID WEST is the longtime owner of Ciderville Music in Powell, Tennessee. For years he performed on the "Farm and Home Hour," and continues a version of the show at the Ciderville Barn today. His years driving Cas Walker provided him with the best "education" one could ever have.

Beloved in the University of Tennessee's History Department, Emeritus Professor BRUCE WHEELER has written on Cas Walker's role in *Knoxville, Tennessee: A Mountain City in the New South* (University of Tennessee Press, 2005).

BIBLIOGRAPHY

ARCHIVAL MATERIALS

Archives of Appalachia, East Tennessee State University, Johnson City.
  Bradley Reeves Collection.
  Virgil Wacks Collection.
  David West Collection.
Calvin M. McClung Historical Collection, Knox County Public Library, East Tennessee History Center, Knoxville. Multiple holdings related to Cas Walker.
  Biography Clippings Files, four folders.
  Cas Walker Broadcast Collection, 1953–1957.
  Vic Weals Collection: Interviews with Cas Walker, 1979.
University of Tennessee Libraries, Digital Collections.
  Charlie Daniels Editorial Cartoon Collection.

BOOKS

Allen, Ronald R. *From Cas Walker's to Downtown Hawkers*. Knoxville, TN: Self-published, 2008.
Jenkins, Ray. *The Terror of Tellico Plains: The Memoirs of Ray H. Jenkins*. Knoxville: East Tennessee Historical Society, 1978.
Walker, Cas. *My Life History: A True Living Legend*. Knoxville, TN: Self-published, 1993.
———. *White Caps and Blue Bills*. Knoxville, TN: Self-published, 1974. Revised version of *The Sevier County White-Caps* by Tom Davis.
Wheeler, Bruce. *Knoxville, Tennessee: A Mountain City in the New South*. 2nd edition. Knoxville: University of Tennessee Press, 2005.

NEWSPAPERS

Knoxville News Sentinel, 1922–90. Online at Newsbank, https://infoweb-newsbank.com.ezproxy.knoxlib.org/resources/search/.

Knoxville Journal, 1932–91, Microfilm. Calvin M. McClung Historical Collection, Knox County Public Library System, East Tennessee History Center, Knoxville.
Metro Pulse, 1991-2014. Owned by E.W. Scripps. No archives maintained.
Watchdog (Knoxville, TN), 1969–81. Calvin M. McClung Historical Collection, Knox County Public Library System, East Tennessee History Center, Knoxville. Also, issues for years 1974–81 available on eight rolls of 35mm microfilm, Tennessee State Library and Archives, Nashville.

INDEX

Page numbers in **BOLDFACE** refer to illustrations; page numbers in *italics* refer to biographical sketches.

A & P (grocery store), 16, 51, 75
accordion, 79
Acuff, Roy, 58
Acuff family, 55
Alger, Horatio, 7
American Civil Liberties Union, 128
arthritis, 33
Asbury Acres (convalescent home), 175
Ashe, Victor, 93, 122–23, 159–60, 180, 186, 189, *193*
athlete's foot, 32–33
Atkins, Chet, 58

Bailey, Dan ("Curly Dan," Danny), 55, 59, 164
Baker, Carter G., 52
balloon advertising, 21–22
Bean, Betty, 7–8, 32, 43, 55, 68, 90–91, 93–95, 105, 164–65, 169–70, 173–74, 186–91, *193*
Bean, John "LeRoy Mercer," 188, 190
Bean, Ralph, 188, 190
Beaver, Pappy Gube, 177
beer trucks, 151
Berry, Fred, 128, 138
Bingham, Lula M., 85–86
Bishop, Walker, 123–24
Blanchard, Lowell, 68–69, 79

Bledsoe, Wayne, 68–70
Blue Band (Walker brand), 16, 56, 59, 67, 184, 187
Blue Bills, 1, 7–8
Booker, Robert (Bob), 17, 19–20, 43, 76, 97–98, 125–27, 129–31, 146–47, 149, *193*
Boone, Claude, 30, 55–56
Bragg, James, 15–16, 20, 22–23, 27, 41–42, 53, 60, 66–67, 75, 98, 121, 133–34, *193*
Breeden, Blanche, 173–74
Brewster, Bud (Franklin), 59, 64–65
Brewster, Willie G., 59, 64–65
bribes, 147–48
Brownlow, Parson, 175
Bulloch, Jim, 137–38
Butcher, C. H., 186, 188–89
Butcher, Shirley, 188
Butler, Carl, 70
Butler, Jesse W., 165
Butler, Pearl, 69–70

Calhoun, John C., 174
Carmichael, Stokely, 124
Carson, James, 59
Carter family, 55
Carter Sisters, 58
Cas Walker Band, **110**
"Cas Walker Farm and Home Hour" (WBIR), 2, 40, 55–56, **57**, 66, 68–70, 72, 130, 185, 188–89, 191
cats, 138–41

197

Channel 10. *See* WBIR (TV)
chickens, 1, 25–27, 35, 44, 155
Ciderville, 3, 55, 171, 174
civil rights, 126, 128
Clay, Henry, 174
cloggers, 55, 68, 187
clothing, need for, 86, 88
coffee, 16, 35, 56, 59, 184
Cole, T. Edward, 150–51
Colonial Heights Nursing Home, 174
comics, 98
Communism, opposition to, 121–23, 125–28
Cooper, Ed, 12–13
Cooper, J. S. (Jack, "Cadillac Jack"), 2–3, **92**, 96, 103, **104**, 105, 149–52, 154, 167–69, 189
Cooper, Jimmy ("Popcorn"), 96, 103
Cope, Rowdy, 36, 47, 61–62, 137, 177, *193*
Correll, David, 179
country image, 2–3, 8, 23–24, 55, **57**, 66–67, 170, 181, 187
Cupp, Mrs. John, 87–88

Dalton, Howard, 32
Dalton, Stevie, 32
Dance, Jack, 2
Daylight Savings Time, opposition to, 105
Dempster, George, 94, 98, 129
desegregation, 127, 129
dial-a-message calls, 123–24
dogs, 3–4, 25, 35, 67, 82, 133–38, 140–41, 154, 156–57, 185, 190
Donaldson, Sherman, 130
Dougherty, W. P. Boone, 150–51, **153**
Dunaway, Wade E., 152
Duncan, John, Sr., 108–9, 129
Dwarshuis, Becky Orange, 50–51, 61–62, 77–78, 81–82, *193*

Eddie's Auto Parts, 188
elections, 93–94, 97–99, 101–3, 128, 151, 167–68
Ellenburg, Henry, 154
Emery, Ralph, 72

Everett, Larry, 162
Everly, Don, 69
Everly, Ike, 69
Everly, Margaret, 69
Everly, Phil, 69
Everly Brothers, 2, 55–56, 68–70
ex-convicts, 50–51, 89

Federal Communications Commission (FCC), 108–9, 123
feelings, hurt, 87–88
Finley, Louie Chester, 28–29
flood sale, 30–31, 185
food, freshness of, 17–18
Ford, Linda, 139–41
Ford, Roe, 190
Foster, Steven, 162, 166
Freeberg, Ernest, 4–5
Full Cry (magazine), 133, 135
funeral aid, 76, 78–79

Gaddis, Dave, 162, **163**
Gannon, Ernie, 20
Gelliam, Hattie, 86
Gibson, Don, 58–59, 68
Gibson, Jimmy, 105
gondolas, 106
Grand Ole Opry, 59, 70, 72
greasy pole, 62–65
Green, Bob, 127
groceries: bagging technique, 48; prices of, 17–18, 124
grocery store: in Bearden, **14**; on Broadway, 78; on Chapman Highway, 39–45, 190; on Clinton Highway, 21–22; at Five Points, 130; in Fountain City, 188; on Magnolia Avenue, 1, 17, 53, **118**; at Market Square, 139; on McCullough Avenue, 17; on Vine Street/Avenue, 9, **10**, 11–12, 26, 91, 93; on Walker Blvd., 138–41; on Western Avenue, 1, 17, **46**, 130
grocery stores: arrangement of, 15–17, 25; in black community, 17, 130–31; boycott

of, 124, 126, 129–30; cleanliness of, 18; fires in, **118**, **158**; location of, 1–2, 17, 100, 130–31, 155, 188

Hammond, Walter, 84
Harber, Tyler, 191
Harper, Harold, 59
Harris, Roger, 149–52
Harvey, Eddie, 188
Hawk, Diana, 79
hemorrhoids, 32–33
Highlander Folk Center, 121–28
Hodge, Joshua S., 3–4, 129–31
horses, 3, 47, 91, 137; racing of, 22–23
Horton, Myles, 125–27
housing, rebuilt, 83–84, 89
Hurst, Don, 89

IGA (grocery store), 129
Internal Revenue Service, 160
Irwin, John Rice, 174–75
Ivory, William, 145

Jean, Bennie Wallen, 12, 29–30, 41, 48–49, 135–37, 169, *193*
Jemima, Aunt, 29
Jenkins, Ray, 159–61
jobs needed, 87–89
Johnson, Mrs. Roy, 105
Johnson, O. C. ("Little Cas"), 93, 95, 170
Johnson, Walker, 39
Johnson Mountain Boys, 70
Jones, Matthew A., Sr., 128
Julian, Toby ("Post-Hole"), 96

Kesley, Howard N., **116**
Kessell, W. Dwight, **116**
Key, Clyde W., 160–61
King, Martin Luther, Jr., 126
Knox County Health Department, 138–41
Knox County Housing Authority, 2, 153–54
Knox County Humane Society, 139
Knox County Welfare Department, 91

Knoxville, Tennessee (Wheeler and McDonald), 94–95
Knoxville, TN, 1, 3–5, 56; desegregation of, 127, 129, 131; and music, 58–59, 69; TV in (besides Cas Walker), 39, 65, 80
Knoxville City Council, 94, 106, 144, 186; fight in, **92**, 93, 95, 103, **104**, 105
Knoxville *Journal*, 58–59, 94, 143, 186; Milk Fund of, 75, 90–91, 169–70, 173, 175
Knoxville *News-Sentinel*, 143–45, 169, 173
Knoxville school board, 149, 151–52, 167–68
Kroger (grocery store), 17–19, 75, 129, 169

labor organizing, opposition to, 126
Lane, Odell Cas (nephew), 2, 91, 102, 124–28, 169, 173
lawyers, 84–85, 159–61
Lee, McAfee, 160–61
Leopper, Lynn, 185
Life (magazine), 93, 95, 103, 105, 189
Lindsay, Powell, 123–24
liquor, 97–99
liquor interests, 168
loans, 82–83, 85–86, 163, 166
Lobetti, Mose, 151
"Lonesome Pine Boys, The," 70
Long, Huey, 187
Long John, 188
Louvin Brothers, 72
Loveday, Bob, 91
Lutrell, Robert (Bob), 23–25, 33–34, 135, *193*
Lynn, Loretta, 62, 73

Madrick, Cal, 145
Maples, Bill, 139–41, 154–57
margarine, 23–24
Mathis, Larry, 16, 28, 30, 39, 41, 59–60, 64–65, 67–68, 83, 122, 134, 166–67, 181, 185, *194*
Maybelle, Mother, 58
McCarthy, Joseph, 123
McClary, Jacquelyn B., 152, 154
McClellan, Vicky, 141

Index   199

McCord, Keith, 151, 169
McDonald, Michael, 94–95, 191
McKinney, Walter, Jr., 162, 166
meat, 17–18, 21, 35, 187
medical help needed, 85–87
Metro Pulse, 170
"Midday Merry-Go-Round, The," 58, 69, 79
Miller, Art, 150
Mink, Ken, 71–73
Morrell, Gene, 162, **163**
Morrison, Jerry, **132**
Motavou, Zimbabwe, 129–31
Mull, J. Bazzel (Basil), 20–21, 187
Mull, Mrs., 21, 187
murder, 37
Murphy College, 8–9
Museum of Appalachia, 174–75
music: country, 48, 67–73, 167, 184; opinions on, 67–68, 167; rock 'n' roll, 3, 58, 68–70, 166–67, 187
My Life History (Walker), 8–9, 11, 19, 21, 25–27, 32, 44–45, 49–50, 63, 145–46, 163–64

Nashville, and music, 58, 69–70
Newton, Robert, 59

O'Dell, Digger, **38**, 39–45, 190
Orange Bowl Queen, **113**
Osborne Brothers, 72

pancakes, 29
Parton, Dolly, 2, 4, 55–56, 61–65, 68, 70–72, 173, 191
Pennington Gap, VA, 2, 30–31, 35, **158**, 185
Pierce, Bo, 18–19, 42, 96, 99, 103, 106, 138, 171, *194*
pigs, 139
police raids, 127
political correctness, 29
possums, 20, 22, 191
Presley, Elvis, 45, 58, 145–46, 166, 190
produce, 15, 18, 25

Quarles, Mr. (U.S. Marshal), 161

raccoons, 3, 20, **132**, 133–34, **136**, 137–38, 156, 173, 190
race mixing, 126–27
race relations, 147
racial insensitivity, 29, 130–31
Ragsdale, Mike, 191
Ramsey, Fred, 145
rats, 138–39, 141
Rector, Red, 55, 59, 66
Redbone (dog), 135–36
Reece, Carroll, 72
Reeves, Bradley, 52, 58, 60, 65, 71, 131, 176–77, 181, 183–84, *194*
Ritchie, Robert, **164**
roach killer, 67
"Robert, little," 59
Roberts, Buster, 91
Roberts, Milton E., **116**
Rogers, Leonard Reid, 106, 127
Rose, Julia, 171
Ross, Jeff, 56
Routh, Bill, 19, 145
Routh, Greg, 19
Routh, John C. (Casey), 145

Savage, Peggy, 173, 175
Scalf, Major Temple, 52–53
Sear, Charla, 34
Severance, Phyllis, 151
Sevier County, TN, 1, 7
Sharp, Jack, v, 40, 96–97, 143, 182–83, 194
Sharp, Mrs. Squire, 86–87
shears, 18–20, 96, 190–91
shoplifting, 36–37
Shuler, Jane Bandy, 51–52
"silk stocking crowd," 58, 94, 96
slogans, 18–22, 96, 191
Smith, Carl, 68–69, 72
Smith, Fred, 59, 64–66
Smith, Hubert O'Dell. *See* O'Dell, Digger
snakes, 40–41, 44, 133

Stout, Sylvia, 190
Strange, Johnny, 186–87, 190
Supraderm (Superderm) Salve, 32–34, 171

teachers, 80
telephone harassment, 123–24
Tennessee Archive of Moving Image and Sound (TAMIS), 58
Tennessee Public Service Commission, 123
Tennessee Valley Advertising Agency, 4, 48, 51–52, 140, 152, 154–56, 168–69
Testerman, Kyle, 101–2
Thomas, Blanch M., 88
Tindell, Billy, 166, 188
Tindell, Harry, 188
Tindell, Mary H., 130, 162–64, **164**, 165–66, 188
Tipton, Catlett, 8
Toole, Bobby ("Coaldaddy"), 186–88, 190
truck accident, 187–88
Tucker, Julia, 107, 148–52, 168, 182, 194
Tyree, Mary Pat, **100**
Tyree, Randy, 2, **100**, 100–103, 106–8, 128–29, 183, 194

underwear, 9
utilities needed, 88

Venable, Sam, 184–85
vote-buying and manipulation, 97–99, 101–3, 156

Wagner, Porter, 62
wagon, delivery, 9, 11–12, 91
Walker (Matorin), Wilma June (daughter), 2, 91, 94, **112**, 157, 173
Walker, Annie Stephens (mother), 1, **6**, 7
Walker, Ben H., 18, 49, 59, 61, 78–79, 147, 182, 194
Walker, Carl, 78
Walker, Cas (Orton Caswell): and adoption arrangement, 81–82; and Alzheimer's alleged, 50, 90, 170–71, 173, 175, 186; and animosity toward enemies, 144, 151, 182, 184; and assault charge, 162–65, 188; birth of, 1, 7, 155; and black employees, 126, 130–31; and blooper tape, 71; books by, 8, 82; burial of, **119**, 186, 190; and cars, 137, 181, 190; and changing bandages, 77–78; as city councilman, 2, 93–94, **116**, 121, 128, 156, 186, 188–89; and class consciousness, 148; and cleanliness lacking, 134; as coal miner, 1, 8, 12, 31, 34, 50, 91, 93, 107, 148, 155; as common man, 75, 156, 160–61, 180–82 (*see also* country image); and Communism, 121–23, 189; and control issues, 107; as coon hunter, 2–4, 23, 32, 55, 90, 103, **132**, 133–35, 138, 154–56, 159, 171; death of, 3, 177, 184; dictates newspaper article, 144–45; and dog sales, 67, 82, 135–37, 185; and education, 8, 159, 161, 182; and employees of, 47–51, 126, 130–31, 135–37, 169; and fighting, 8–9, 11–13, 36, 49–50, **92**, 103, **104**, 105; and firing non-employees, 52–53; and funeral flowers, 76, 131; generosity of, 75–76, 79–80, 82–83, 95, 175, 179; and God, 76–77; and grocery stores, 1, 3, 8–9, **10**, 11–12, **14**, 15–18, 48–49, 152, 154–55, 160, 169, 173, 181, 184; and helping people, 76–79, 81, 83–88, 160–61, 179; and Highlander Center opposition, 123–25, 127–28; and hospital donations, 75; and hurt feelings, 87–88; illness of, 173–77; and job interviews, 51–52; letters to, 84–89, 105; and libel cases, 143–44, 147, 149–52, 154–56, 167–69; as mayor, 2, 93–94, **95**, **113**, 144, 156; and media, 2–5, 55, 65, 93; and medications, 65, 171, 173; as millionaire, 69, 76, 137, 149, 152, 156, 173, 177, 180–81, 184; motivated by money-making, 75–76, 83, 131; and musicians, 2–3, 55–56, 58–62, 67–68, 71–73, 171, 175, 181, 184, 191; and newspapers, 2–4, 58–59, 72, 100, 108, **142**, 143–52, 154–56, 159, 167–69, 171, 180, 184,

Walker, Cas (*continued*)
188; use of nicknames by, 3, 96; and nursing home, 90, 159, 170, 173–75, 186; office of, 97; opinions about, v, 3, 5, 67–68, 147–49, 174, 179–85, 191; and opposition to change, 94, 101, 105–8, 121–23, 129–30, 181–84, 186, 189; photos of, **frontispiece, 6, 31, 54, 57, 74, 92,** 93, 95, **95,** 100, 104, 105, **110–20, 132, 136, 142, 153, 161, 163, 172, 178,** 189; plain-spokenness of, 137, 180–81; and policemen, 42, 100, 135, 140, 143, 149, 152, 167, 186; and politics, 2–5, 58, 67–68, 71, 91, 93, 95, 101–3, 108–9, 134, 143–44, 147–48, 151–52, 156, 160, 165, 167–68, 181–84, 187–88; and power, 107, 182; and power lost by, 166–68, 189; and power of the press, 149; property holdings of, 1, 8, 18, 93, 155–56, 160; and publicity, 1, 3–4, 12, 15–16, 19–35, 39–45, 55–56, 59–60, 63, 65–69, 71–72, 84, 93, 95–97, 103, 105, 108, 139, 146, 152, 155, 171, 174–75, 181, 183–84, 186, 190; and racism, 128–29, 131; and radio, 2, 58, 65, 69, 71, 85–86, 191; recall of, 2, 94; and segregation/desegregation, 121, 124, 126, 128–31; speaks at UT, 34–35, 40, 134–35; and tax evasion trial, **114–15,** 159–61; and TV, 2–3, 22, 27–29, 37, 43, 55, **57,** 59–62, 65–69, 71–72, 79, 84, 89, 96, 108–9, 130, 138, 143, 147, 159, 162–63, 165–67, 171, 176, 185–87; and violence, 170; and water fluoridation, 4, 105, 121–22, 186, 189; as young man, 1, 7–9, 12

Walker, Thomas (father), 1, **6,** 7
Walker, Virginia Grantham (Ginnie) (wife), 2, 21, 32–33, 76, 90–91, 94, 101, **112,** 154, 157, 159, 170–71, **172,** 173, 186, 190

Walker family, photo of, **6, 112**
Warner, Carl, 17, 80, 99, 143–44, 147–48, *194*
Watchdog (newspaper), 3–4, 100, 108, **142,** 143–52, 154–56, 159, 167–69, 171, 180, 184, 188
WATE (TV), 2, 28, 65, 108, 171
water fluoridation, 4, 105, 121–22, 186, 189
watermelons, 20, 22, 29, 130–31, 185, 187, 191
Watson, Hal, 71
WBIR (TV), 2, 28, 40, 56, **57,** 65, 69, 71, 79, 108, 162–63, 165–66, 171, 185, 188
Webb, Robert, 152
Webster, Ronald, 166
Webster Brothers, 59
West, David, 31, 42–43, 55–56, 58–59, 60–62, 76–77, 81–84, 89, 171, 174, 179–80, *194*
Wheeler, Bruce, 9, 17–18, 20, 43, 66, 94–96, 103, 122, 134–35, 191, *194*
whiskey, 97
White Caps, 1, 7–8
White Caps and Blue Bills of Sevier County (Walker), 8
White Store (grocery store), 17, 53, 75, 129
Wiedemann, Jack, 108–9, 182
Wilds, Honey, 55, 59, 189
Wing, Jerry, 66
Winn Dixie (grocery store), 146
Wiser, Don, 186–88
WIVK (radio), 48, 58, 61, 91
WKXT (TV), 91
WKXV (radio), 65
WNOX (radio), 58
World's Fair, 2, 107–8, 139, 183, 189
WROL (radio), 58, 65
WSM (Nashville radio), 58
WTSK (TV), 65
Wynn, Pleas, 8